The Fat Jesus

The Fat Jesus

Christianity and Body Image

LISA ISHERWOOD

SEABURY BOOKS
an imprint of
Church Publishing Incorporated, New York

Published in 2007 by
Darton, Longman and Todd Ltd
1 Spencer Court
140–142 Wandsworth High Street
London SW18 4JJ

First published in the United States in 2008 by
Seabury Books
An imprint of Church Publishing, Incorporated
445 Fifth Avenue
New York, New York 10016

www.churchpublishing.com

ISBN: 978-1-59627-094-7

A catalog record for this book is available from the Library of Congress

5 4 3 2 1

Printed and bound in Great Britain

The reign of God is a warm, fleshy, all encompassing body with enough spare flesh for all to be nourished.[1]

Contents

Contents

Introduction:

Heaven is a room full of fat women laughing!

Liberation theologies have been around for a long time now and feminist liberation theologies for almost as long. During their history they have questioned the very essence of the Christian faith from Christology to ethics, through church history to hermeneutics. The results have been incredible and the world that has opened up has been one of many colours and ever unfolding layers of lived reality. We have seen what a difference a black Christ can make not only to the christological debate itself but to the ethics that inevitably unfold from liberation christological reflection. The rainbow of Christs it has been possible to imagine through the use of liberation methods have made accessible a wealth of lived reality and continued to broaden the theological world. As Christ is differently imagined so too the theological world has to question itself. Slowly with each emerging Christ the theological construction begins to shift and what was once viewed as beyond change, as in place before all time, takes more inclusive and creative turns. We have Asian Christs, Latin American Christs both male and female, queer Christs and gay and lesbian Christs, Christ Sophia and disabled Christs. The list appears endless, but there is one notable absentee, the Fat Jesus, or the corpulent Christ. When I did a web search I found that the only Fat Jesus that exists is a Cuban cigar! What is it in our contemporary world, I wondered, that made a Fat Jesus undesirable? This simple question has raised many more and led me into a world that has made me sad, angry and, at moments, hopeful.

I have been asked why I would even ask the question about a Fat Jesus, but as a liberation theologian whose work is based in ideas of radical incarnation I have to ask it. For me Christianity is about the flesh and blood reality of people's lives in which co-creation and co-redemption are lived out, so it follows that all manner of embodiment and embodied experience is a further unfolding of the divine/human reality that we live. Of course this understanding of Christianity has also made me very suspicious about things we take as 'normal' in theology and society. We are living at a time when fat phobia is at its height and to question this is seen as a sin, because the rhetoric is about making people healthy and caring for their well-being. When we look at the reality we see that there is a great deal of prejudice about fat people that does not speak of concern and respect – there is a mismatch in the rhetoric. Recently it has been suggested that fat children should be taken into care for their own good, because it was neglect by their parents that allowed them to become so large. In addition we are bombarded with programmes showing us young people being sent to camps because they are over-weight. 'Fat Camp' is one such programme which has a regime akin to the worst excesses of boot camp. These young people cry and show signs of psychological distress, but because they are fat they are supposed somehow to deserve it. We are told overweight women may not conceive, and it has been reported very recently that overweight women were not employed by high street banks as they gave the wrong image.[1] As a theologian I believe that much that we experience in the secular world has deep theological and religious roots and so by turning to the Christian heritage of these in the West I am not at all surprised to see that size carries with it a gendered rhetoric about moral goodness and sanctity. Under this theology flesh on women has always been dubious while monks have always been great cooks and winemakers! As we shall see, gender makes an embodied difference in our Christian heritage and in our everyday lives in the present.

There is usually a combination of events, almost always in the lives of women, that makes me think I want to spend the time researching and writing in a certain area. For this book a number of things came together against a personal background of being categorised due to size. Even as a younger woman on an athletic scholarship I was always considered overweight, against whose standards I was never sure. Since researching this book, the question of who decides what is acceptable, particularly for women, has become clearer. Despite the experiential nature of feminist theology, if my story alone was the basis of the book it would not lead to very useful theology. However, there has been a very lucrative but worrying development in the area of conservative theology particularly in the United States. The 'Slim For Him' programme is a billion-dollar industry which extols the religious virtue of being slim and frames fat as sin. This movement is particularly popular with women and becoming slim for Jesus appears to be almost part of what good Christian womanhood implies in some circles. Of course we should not be too surprised at this as there have always been women throughout the history of Christianity who have given up eating for Jesus. I will look at this issue in Chapter 2 as it is not at all clear whether we can make links between the approach of our foresisters and our contemporary sisters who appear to believe themselves more lovable if they fade away.

'Slim For Him' would perhaps be less of a concern for me if it was not for the ever increasing number of deaths from anorexia that are sweeping through our world. With 1 in 5 young women affected, we are really at crisis point, yet the world does not appear to notice. We have young women walking amongst us whose bones are on display, they have dark shades in their faces, and they walk slowly, only swallow bits of bread and have white spittle on their lips. They move like the living dead of concentration camps and there is no medical reason for this – they are not stricken with a wasting disorder and they do not live in countries where food is hard to find. Should we be holding crisis talks? The future is being diminished through the death of so many of these bright and able young women – through the suicide of young women. In 2002 a web search revealed 650,000 sites that were to do with eating disorders, 415,000 of which were related to anorexia. They had names such as 'Dying to be Thin', 'Anorexia Nation' and 'Stick Figures'.[2]

In truly religious style there are 10 commandments for anorexics posted on the websites, called '0 Thin Commandments'. The heart of this guide for life is that you can never be too thin and you have to buy clothes which make you appear as thin as possible. You must understand that 'being thin is more important than being healthy'; 'thou shall not eat without feeling guilty'; 'thou shall not eat fattening foods without punishing yourself afterwards'; and 'what the scales says is the most important thing'.[3] A truly religious frame, especially as the outcome of all this is something that would make the Church Fathers proud: willpower and success in controlling the body. These websites that make perfect sense to those who create them and provide a supportive community may leave the rest of us a little mystified. As a feminist liberation theologian I find myself asking what has happened that these young women and girls can not imagine their lives without a life-threatening condition? What has happened that they can not engage with their desire and imagination, that these have to be reduced through limiting lifestyles that affect the body and the mind, that make them lethargic, weak and ill? And, crucially, what is it in the world that allows so much of this behaviour to go unnoticed, or even to be applauded, and what is it that makes it so hard for our young women to live life in abundance on this planet at this time?

Food and the Body of Christ

As a body theologian I have some ideas already in answer to this. It is difficult for women to be fully embodied under patriarchy, as has been demonstrated in works relating to sexuality, and it may be that food is seen as just as physical and sensual and so to be restricted in women in a way it is not with men. The rhetoric of over-sensual women can, I believe, extend to eating and the enjoyment of food by women. The whole idea of sensuous enjoyment can set off alarm bells in many Christian circles for both sexes. Of course there is a paradox here, since the Messianic Banquet, which is thought to be at the end for all, is heralded through the eucharistic meal shared among believers. Christianity like many religions has in this respect understood the powerful way in which food acts as a language of memory: in celebrating with bread and wine in memory of Christ we are drawing believers into a fully embodied experience. They take into themselves that which they are remembering and that in turn acts as a series of ongoing memories, their own and that of the generations before them, all of whom shared that same meal with that same memory. Catholics have always believed that a profound change takes place at the Eucharist, not only to the elements themselves but also to those who ingest them; they become drawn into a totality of life that is both public and private. Those who share this table are asked to accept a set of radical values that are in opposition to those of the world and the respectable and established order of things. Those assembled in community around the table are in an act of profound friendship which extends to the whole of the created order. More than the brain is connected here – the whole body is engaged. In the Eucharist food is not just what we do as part of a celebration, it is the core of what it is we are remembering, engaging in – ingesting. I would hate to think that this powerful tool of remembering and embodying could be turned into the ultimate contemporary food ideal, that is to say, heavenly satisfaction and no calories!

Of course we should not forget that we live in a western industrialised world where obesity is also a reality. It is estimated that almost 50 per cent of the population in the UK, Canada and the USA are classed as obese. We do, however, need to be mindful that the obese classification starts at something like 15 to 20 pounds over the chart, charts that vary and are not always medically sanctioned. Nevertheless the increase in children's weight over a 15-year period has been estimated at a 92 per cent increase in boys and a 57 per cent increase in girls.[4] Interestingly these figures, which I have taken from a health website, go straight into calculating the financial cost of obesity which it estimates at $3.5 billion in care for diabetes, hypertension and heart disease. These calculations are missing from the same website in relation to anorexia, and there is of course a cost attached there too. It does note that health-care professionals are slow to address the issue of obesity until it is accompanied by health problems. The recommendations that are from the Surgeon General in the USA for combating childhood obesity are splendid in intention and rather apolitical, that is to say he recommends that there are low-fat options in school meals but does not mention that fast food chains have the franchise for many schools and are in fact creating what they call more cost-effective options, which are actually bigger portions for the same money. It seems then that half the western world is starving itself while the other half is overweight, while beyond the western world there is simply often not enough food to go round. There would seem to be an issue here then.

From a feminist perspective there may be something to alert us to how food and women interact through a slight glance at the history of Christian women and food. Unlike our Jewish sisters we have been given very little ritual significance in our food preparation. In Judaism when the Temple fell and with it the sacrificial altar it was replaced by the set table, the community fellowship. This has meant that Jewish women through the food rituals carried out at their family tables actually perform and maintain culture in everyday life as well as through preparations for holy days. Of course for Christian women the picture is reversed. What started as a house fellowship movement then grew and moved out into churches and cathedrals. This led to the diminishment of women's role in ceremony and thus their reduced role in relation to the religiously symbolic nature of food. It may be then that Christian and Jewish women have very different experiences when it comes to the symbolic nature of food and their sex. That interesting question is, though, beyond the scope of this book. Whatever we may decide in relation to that question it remains true to say that food is a cultural experience and of course men and women under patriarchy have very different experiences of culture.

This is not a book about eating-disordered people and helpful therapies for them; it is not even a book about abstinence for Jesus. It is rather a protest at the wrong thinking that causes the misery, exclusion and even death of thousands who can not find a way to love their bodies and to live life in abundance. As a theological project, then, it is rooted in the incarnational theology that is the centre of all my work,[5] an incarnation that is erotic, sensuous and powerful; one that urges us forward to relationality and flourishing, to life in abundance. It is as much a sexual theology as anything and it is certainly an obscene Christ[6] who will emerge. This is not a Christology of denial and narrow boundaries: it is one of embrace and expansion that wilfully wishes to move the edges. It is a theology/Christology that takes as read that radical politics is not an added extra to an internal relationship with an ethereal Christ but, rather, radical countercultural politics is the skin we put on, the Christ we incarnate. In this book then, the radical living, the skin we put on, that we are searching for, is to be found in incarnated embodied women glorying in their divine fleshiness, women being happy and creative in the skin in which they find themselves. After all, it is this skin that is the divine reality they live. Incarnation tells us that our bodies are our homes, that is to say our divine/human desiring dwelling-places, therefore our christological journey is homeward, to the fullness of our incarnation, the co-redemptive, co-creative reality of our fleshy heaven.[7] Part of what I am hoping will emerge from this research is a Christ of womanly abundance and it will be interesting to examine the ethical implications of such an emergence. It is the world we create through christological ponderings that are of extreme importance and not the metaphysical workings of essences and hypostatic unions that exercise our minds. So how will the world of women who see themselves as too fat, too small, not small enough look like when this Christ emerges?

Food, self and community

Of course this is not simply a project that finds theological justification through the application of a liberation method. Interestingly the Bible uses food as a sign of many matters of divine importance: it is a sign of love, community and the sacred. This is perfectly in line with the way in which the societies at the time would have understood the significance of food, as we shall see in a moment. For now, though, the question arises that if women are at odds with food through the cultures we have created, are they too at odds with the love, community and sacredness of life itself? If women are not honoured guests at those tables of love, community and the sacred, where are they to find full humanity? Understanding incarnation as I do, then, the politics of eating are as important as any other matter – they are a theological issue. Eating, like any other human activity, becomes an incarnational matter too, one that enables or restricts our divine becoming and the glorious explosion of our dunamis, the raw and dynamic energy that is the divine within us, through our embodied, lived realities. Of course, as already mentioned, food – who can eat what and when – has always been a matter of religious and cultural significance and so there seems no better time than now to look at it through feminist incarnational eyes.

We will, however, be looking at one area of human living that has a long and highly complex symbolic heritage. Food and eating have never been simple matters of satisfying hunger. They have always, like other matters of life and death, carried meaning beyond their biological basics. It is this highly symbolic, ritualistic and religious meaning of food that makes it a theological matter. When we look back we see that in primitive society the act of eating symbolised the partaker being eaten by the community and through sharing food becoming a companion (Latin com- + panis, sharing bread), an equal in that society. This simple and basic act then carries historically a great deal of significance – at the heart of it is a notion of sharing, not exchange, in which subjects are born through the powerful symbolism of food.[8] Perception itself is understood as 'taking in' or 'spitting out' – how we see the world is shaped through this medium. Falk argues that although one became a member of a group self through being eaten by the community and sharing with them, there always remained 'an oral type of self autonomy'[9] – there was subjectivity and group identity in harmony through the primitive understanding of food as a symbol. He goes on to argue that with the collapse of the primitive systems eating changed from an open to a closed activity, from the notion of an eating community to that of a bounded individual eating. In other words there was a huge shift from food and eating being an inclusive community activity to it becoming one that began and ended at the edges of the individual. In this way eating and what was eaten lost their communal symbolism and became signifiers of the worth, merit and general status of the individual, became a sign of the narrowly defined standing of the bounded-in, individual self. Falk points out that in the nineteenth century communal eating reappeared as a sign of Utopia, that is, for a short while it regained its egalitarian communal symbolism. Of course the Christian Church can argue that the eating community never went away within its walls since the eucharistic meal has always been there. There are great symbolic differences between the

Roman Catholic and Protestant traditions in relation to the continued significance of the food shared which may, I argue, help to explain the outbreak of 'Slim For Him' programmes in Protestant Christianity – a phenomenon that is entirely absent in Roman Catholic circles. Of course this may be as much cultural as it is religious, but then which affects which? Norbert Elias has argued that with the shift from eating community to bounded self there also comes an armouring of the self, a level of control that is not seen in eating communities.[10] This also signals a shift from values lying in the community to a new and imaginary inwardness of emotional experience where value may be found, as well as the notion that what is outside may harm this inner depth. The shift in understanding of the symbolic nature of food leads to a crucial shift in the place of the individual in relation to others. There is much more emphasis on the bounded self, which in terms of Christian theology can be understood as personal salvation, the relationship between an ethereal God and the self-defined individual. In broader terms this individual sense also disconnects people from the wider community and leaves them vulnerable, indeed primed to be genocidal consumers. I mean their bounded selves need things and the cost is not counted – there is no 'eating community' to which they are attached, and so only a bounded self to be served.

There is a further shift which may throw some light on this research. Falk suggests that 'the decline of the ritual significance of the meal manifests itself not only in the shift from food to words but also in the informalization of the reciprocal speech acts into conversation in the modern sense of the word'.[11] This understanding of Falk may shed light on the differences between Protestant and Roman Catholic meal significance and that relationship to global capitalism and beyond. This may all be far too great a claim and the research will decide. Protestant theology moves the saving significance from the communal meal to the Word in the book, a speech act, not an embodied act of community, I wonder if it is too much to claim that in such movements as 'Slim For Him', the Word has become informalised as Falk suggests, but to such levels of down-home God-speak that it becomes gibberish that carries no salvific significance at all. 'You are what you eat', which once carried the power of magical transformation

within the eating communities, has now become an individualised sound bite aimed at making us better consumers. The
sensual pleasure of the eating community has, as has been suggested, been replaced by a consumer culture trying to satisfy the
internal emotional depths that have replaced the community – it
may be that the Fat Jesus is that old-fashioned hedonist whose
pleasure in sensual delights would act as a counter to the worst
excesses of global capitalism. The power of religious symbolism
appears to have been lost, but within certain traditions in
Christianity the actions are still there – it may then not be too late
to transform the people of God back into an eating community,
consuming one another in the passionate desire of the divine
incarnate.

One last anecdote before getting on with the book: I have in my
house a lovely statue of the Goddess of Willendorf, that full-
bodied divine female being worshipped for centuries by men and
women alike. During my father's illness there were many carers
coming in and out, the vast majority of them women. Many of
these women would comment on the wonderful shape of the
statue, some would pick her up and run their hands over her
curves with obvious delight – they all agreed she was a wonderful shape, a lovely woman. Most of these women were on diets,
yet hardly any measured up to the girth of the goddess! It is to
those women and many others who do not have the internal
permission to love their bodies that this book is dedicated!

Chapter One

The big question is: who let the skinny girls in?[1]

'Man aspires to clothe in his own dignity whatever he conquers and possesses.' [2]

We appear to be at a time in history when medical advances have made it possible for us in the West to be more optimistic about the fact of embodiment, yet we fail to fully celebrate this new reality. Rather we trivialise our new embodied possibilities through the 'thinness religion which bankrupts us'.[3] It bankrupts us as it makes us despise our bodies because they are not perfect and not indestructible. Of course the bodies that are despised in this way tend to be female bodies since man, like God, is not represented, he represents, he is not gazed at, he gazes, and if he does not like what he sees then culture emerges to please his eye and his psychological needs, to guard his psychic fears – and as always the female body pays the price. These claims will be examined as the book progresses. In size as in other matters that feminist theologians have turned their gaze to it seems that we need to move towards a more generous, dignified and realistic way of living in the body, living in harmony with our flesh and not in a battle against it. This may be in danger of giving us a broader (yes, pun intended) world-view, and where would patriarchy be then?

Those of us who have been considering matters of embodiment for some time will even by now be hearing some familiar sounding ideas, the control of women's bodies being one central theme. Seid and others have wondered if the nineteenth-century obsession with controlling female sexuality has been replaced by the desire to control female size in the twentieth and twenty-first centuries.[4] Certainly we can understand that the female body as a signifier of the state of the nation, the culture, the clan, which we now accept as one way in which it is seen, has to be controlled. It has to show that civilisation is central to any particular group of people; this is why so many bodily behaviours that are not acceptable in women are tolerated in men, indeed at times almost seen as part of 'manly' behaviour, for example belching, spitting and farting. It is the female body that marks the boundaries of a decent society, which is why rape is so common in war as it breaks down the boundaries, insulting and defiling the society, not just the woman, and as such those boundaries have to be policed by patriarchy. The interesting question for feminists today, then, is why it is the slender almost anorexic body that signals the edges of a decent society. The 1960s saw Twiggy introduce us to the girl/woman, the body that at 5 foot 7 inches weighed just 5 stone 7 pounds. We have to wonder how this body replaced Marilyn Monroe in her size-16 glory or before her the rounded bodies of one hundred years ago. We know what has happened: the ideal body is one that is actually only inhabited by about 5 per cent of the female population, which means that the other 95 per cent feel too fat. It is curious, though, that this ideal body is in many ways not a female body at all – to be as slender as that means that all the female secondary sexual characteristics are suppressed; when a person weighs so little there is not much spare for hips, thighs and breasts. This is indeed where plastic surgery comes in and we are given a strange creature, a body that does not have enough natural flesh to signal its femaleness, with large false breasts attached which declare its sexual attractiveness. There is much here for feminist analysis to work with and perhaps for feminist psychologists to have a field day.

We live in a world where female fat is considered to be expendable flesh while we add silicone to women's bodies in order to make them sexy. The reality is that female flesh is sexy, and historically there has been a linking of fatness and fertility which has some medical basis, since fat regulates reproduction. Over one-fifth of women who exercise to shape their bodies have menstrual irregularities and diminished fertility; this kind of hormonal imbalance can lead to ovarian cancer and osteoporosis.[5] The battle against female flesh is in so many ways a battle against nature itself, and this will be familiar ground to feminist theologians who long ago identified the dualism of the Fathers as the ground that diminishes us, in this case literally. The medics who join the war are quick to talk of damage and slow to tell the other side of the dieting culture that we are all part of. In India, for example, even the poorest women eat some 1,400 calories a day while women in the West on the Hilton Head Diet eat 600 calories less then that. This puts them on a lower calorific intake than was calculated by the Nazi regime as necessary to sustain human functioning in concentration camps such as Treblinka. Further, during the war in Holland emergency rations were released when people lost more than 25 per cent of their body weight. This is particularly worrying when we realise that many average-sized women in the West are actually trying to lose that amount of body weight.[6] Even today the UN Health Organisation calculates that a diet of 1,000 calories signals semi-starvation and with it many characteristics of famine such as tension, irritability, preoccupation with food and loss of libido. The famine literature provided by a range of agencies identifies these behaviours as signals of bodies in crisis, yet diet industries associate them, as lack of willpower on the part of individuals, with some kind of psychopathology. Further, there is compelling evidence emerging that links dieting with the development of eating disorders that, as we know, are ravaging the bodies of our young women. Despite the certainty with which we are told fat is unhealthy, the reality is far from certain and many of the additional factors that we find connected with weight have to be calculated in too, such as poverty, class and race. However, it does appear to be arguable that dieting can cause many of the illnesses we are told it prevents, such as hypertension, high cholesterol and diabetes. There is compelling evidence that those who diet and then regain weight have a much higher mortality rate than those who never lose weight. In addition, with the mounting anti-fat feeling in the West fat people are suffering more stress than ever before. This is beginning at an early age with children as young as nine believing they are too fat, and indeed actually hating their bodies.

Skinny girls and fat cats

We should not be surprised at this body hatred by young girls since they are bombarded with images from the media of models and actresses many of whom are already anorexic and surgically altered. Models are now 23 per cent lighter than average women, whereas a generation ago that differential was 8 per cent. This certainly means that these women are not healthy and that they create a very unhealthy image for our young girls. In addition to being of less weight than is healthy their photographs are also air-brushed and computer-altered to enhance their looks. However, people do not take the time to explain to the young that these are not real women at all, but computer and surgical composites of what were once flesh and blood women. They may no longer be real in any meaningful sense but they nevertheless fuel the body images of the young and the not so young, they become the un-attainable by real women, role models of feminine beauty, just as the Virgin Mary was the unattainable role model before them. Just as the Virgin created a tension in us that left us vulnerable to the Church and the ways of male-inspired spiritual direction and the mutilation of body and psyche that often ensued, so these 'not quite women' leave us vulnerable to manipulation by another great phallic patriarchal power, the big business. The more ten-sion we feel, the more we consume in order to ease that tension and the better the market likes it. Our circle of self-destruction is their circle of assured markets and captive psyches. Keeping women in a state of dis-ease with their bodies may be good for the markets but it is very bad for the women and girls. Naomi Wolf comments that the obsession with thinness is not about beauty at all but about female obedience.[7] I wish to argue that this can be understood as both obedience to patriarchy, under-mining female confidence and neutralising women's power in society, and also obedience to the markets, as the cult of thinness works on many different levels and unsurprisingly none really advantage women. It may not be too great an exaggeration to say that for many women being a woman is about believing oneself to be too fat and spending time and energy to monitor that situa-tion. This is certainly a great distraction from taking one's place as an equal in society!

A 1990s survey carried out with girls aged between 9 and 13 in Minnesota found that 64 per cent of them were unhappy with their bodies, but more disturbing still was the high correlation between poor body image and psychological distress.[8] It is interesting to consider why this may be – certainly there will be a level of distress because they do not appear to conform at a time when that is important, but feminist theorists have also suggested that it may be because it is easier to live within the safety of an ideal image than the vulnerability and vitality of female flesh. Living within an image is much easier as an image creates a 'no body' and so we do not have to deal with emotions, desires and passions, since the image has already dealt with this for us and decided what we think and feel. It is fascinating that those who work with young girls are putting this forward as a concrete reason for the rejection of their real bodies – fascinating, because Christian feminist theologians can trace just such a pattern through the history of women and sexuality, one in which the image of ideal women is based on the dispassionate living of the women in those bodies. In the arena of sexuality we have discovered how intrinsic passionate living is to being fully incarnate, and this is no less true in matters of food than it is in matters of sex – it is after all about owning and expressing our joy in life and our desires.

A survey for *Bliss* magazine carried out with 2,000 girls between the ages of 10 and 13 found that one in five of the girls hated their bodies so much they were anorexic or bulimic, while over 25 per cent said they would consider plastic surgery. Of those questioned only 19 per cent were at all overweight, while 67 per cent thought they were, with two out of three of the under-thirteens saying they had already been on a diet. This is particularly alarming when we think that these young girls have not yet fully matured but are already, if the UN Health Organisation figures are to be believed, starving themselves. Will this lead to an eating disorder? Well, it has in the UK where 1.1 million women between the ages of 14 and 25 are affected.[9] One-fifth of those affected are seriously ill and at risk of premature death. While the media is telling us that we are in the middle of a childhood obesity outbreak we also have millions of young girls starving themselves in our midst. And they are communicating with each other through a wide array of websites which encourage their disorder. These sites are not sites to help people understand and overcome this killer condition but rather to encourage and cele- brate this slow suicide. Although, as one site tells us, the success- ful anorexic is the one that does not die, she is the one who embraces the lifestyle and refers to her condition as 'Ana', or 'Mia' if she is bulimic. These pet names hide a terrible truth which is that emaciated bodies are a lifestyle for millions of young women and girls and one that allows them to be part of a group. It is obvious from the websites that these women and girls can not imagine a life without this eating disorder. The sites carry 'inspir- ing' pictures of celebrity anorexics and other pictures of fat women as a warning to people of how they may become if they do not keep at their regimes. It has to be noted that once these sites were discovered in 2002 there was pressure on servers not to provide space. Some responded, but this simply meant that the sites changed server or went more deeply underground with more secretive descriptions. There is ambivalence as to whether they wish others to join or not – some say they would not wish anorexia on their worst enemies while others talk of how to become a good anorexic and advocate it as a worthy way of life. There appears to be an underlying message about being strong and in control which pervades much of the web material.

A large percentage of the girls questioned in the *Bliss* survey, 86 per cent, believed that they would be more attractive to boys and more popular with girls if they were thinner.[10] Of course we know that girls do not live in their bodies in the same way as boys and this is because they are indeed looked at by boys. This seeing of themselves as images in boys' eyes sets up an observing rather than an experiencing of their own bodies, and in this way their bodies become Other to them. They become things to mould and chastise in order to be pleasing to the external gaze. Girls learn at a very young age that the power lies with the one who looks, which leads to a vain effort to regain that control and power through policing of the body. A vain effort, because this is not how it is done – the master's tools will never dismantle the master's house, as Audre Lorde[11] told us, and exerting desire- denying control over one's flesh is the master's main tool. The question of what can be considered 'normal' and, further, what can be seen as empowering for girls growing up in a world aimed at the power of weakness for women will be discussed in a later chapter.

It is worth mentioning at this stage that research carried out in the USA shows that there are race, class and cultural variables in attitudes to size. African American girls are more positive about big bodies but this positive attitude is affected if they are in predominantly white schools. The research appears to show that the anorexic model is a WASP (white Anglo-Saxon Protestant) ideal since American Catholic children and Jewish children are less affected by the diet culture. I wonder if I am on to something when I mention cultures of the disembodied Word versus enfleshed and sensuous liturgical cultures. It is also interesting to note that the positive appreciation of a large African American body is shared by African American men, although both African American and white men say they prefer petite white women. There is some evidence emerging that lesbian children are less affected by the diet culture too. There may be a number of reasons for this, ranging from an embodied rebellion against heterosexist norms, to an outsider experience that sits happily rejecting gender expectations and does not crave the male gaze. Of course the media also exerts less pressure since it is not at all obvious that the women being targeted through advertising and so on are lesbian. Since the huge success of *The L Word*,[12] which features thin, young, glamorous and successful lesbians, there is a concern that the world that young lesbians have been shielded from is creeping up on them. Research suggests that 30 minutes of television is enough to establish negative body images for young girls. The show has been criticised for not in fact representing the lesbian community in its embodied entirety.

It has been strongly argued that it is the sexualisation of the anorexic body that is affecting girls at a younger and younger age. When three-year-olds are being targeted for strapless bras and shiny lip gloss it is no wonder that by the age of nine or younger these girls are over-conscious of their bodies as candy for the male gaze. Fashion has always been a way to present women in a passive way to an active gaze and it is alarming that this is now the case for three-year-olds. These young and developing bodies are under pressure to conform, and that may include a mutilation of their bodies as well as an adorning. We are teaching our young girls obsession with the body rather than passionate embodiment, but then heteropatriarchy does not want passion-ate embodiment in women – it thrives on women dwelling insecurely in their skins. Capitalism also requires the kind of discontent that disembodied living generates in order that it may generate what makes it happy, bigger and bigger markets for more and more unnecessary goods.

The anti-fat prejudice that is sweeping the nation is also having an effect on social mobility for fat people in a way not known to date. It is more correct to say 'for fat women', since men appear to be less affected by this prejudice in terms of jobs and university entrance. It appears that obesity, which was once thought to be the result of poverty amongst other factors, is now emerging as the cause of poverty. As a feminist liberation theologian I have to be concerned when the quality of life of women is being affected by how they wish to manifest in the world. As always then we begin to see that questions of embodiment carry with them economic and social questions too. They also carry questions of self-esteem and the love that women need to feel for their embodied realities if they are to have life in abundance. What we also see is that women are not encouraged to live in their bodies, and with this disembodiment comes a rupture in our psyches, believing as we do that we are burdened with flesh that is not our friend. The feminist theological issue of women and size is not an easy side swipe at culture and fashion alone. It is a sincere and heartfelt challenge to the way in which women have been cast out from home, the home of their bodies, and placed in combat with themselves. It is a challenge to the notion that the bodies of women are commodities either to be dieted or to be paraded and adorned.

Nelle Morton[13] advised us all those years ago that the journey for women is home and that was never truer than in relation to our own empowered embodiment. We have been cast adrift from our own enfleshed power for too long and the regulation of size as well as sexuality has been one way in which this alienation has been performed upon us. Home is not just a nice and cosy construct in Morton's theology; it is rather the very beingness of who we are, the place from which we can begin to act in the world in such a way as to change it. It is the power and possibility of living in one's skin, as I would see it the place from which incarnation redeems and co-creates – no cosy and safe space, but a necessary space if we are ever to live the fullness of our divine human natures. In the light of this understanding the issue of women and size is far more than shape and poundage; it becomes theological politics and redemptive praxis. When we are attacked in our skins as women so often are under the rigours of patriarchal constructs, it is nothing less than a profound and shocking act of blasphemy. Traditional theology has not helped women in this respect, since it too has had a love/hate attitude to the female body stemming largely from its reliance on Aristotelian philosophy and its pervasive dualism. This dualism splits the body between flesh and spirit with the greatest value placed on spirit and the body viewed as something to be suspicious of and certainly controlled through discipline. When the body is that of a saint or martyr it is worshipped; when it is real female flesh it is held in contempt as not sufficiently in the image of God to warrant a second thought. This religious dualism has, I believe, infected our secular world so that what we see today in relation to the female body goes deep into our psyches, psyches affected by the destructive split thinking of dualism. There also appears to be a fear of female flesh and while there may be many psychological theories in relation to this, many of which I would agree with, I also believe that Eve lurks LARGE as the primal mother who dared to eat, to taste, to enflesh.

As we begin to understand that the question of women and size is not as straightforward as we may have thought, that is it is not simply a question of health and well-being, we are able to see that power and the politics of gender are lurking not too far beneath the surface. As theologians we also begin to see that these issues are deeply embedded and have probably been derived from a body-denying dualism. As Wolf tells us, anorexia is not personal it is political: if 60 per cent of college women can not eat then we can hardly simply say that 60 per cent of families are dysfunctional and produce psychologically disturbed daughters.[14] The analysis, she insists, has to go beyond the notion of individual moral weakness and families that nurture it. For Wolf semistarvation in women produces many cultural effects, and it is these we have to expose: chiefly, semi-starvation makes the women who suffer it physically and psychologically debilitated; the desire for food makes the successful woman feel a failure; and the need to be thin takes a great deal of female energy. The thin ideal is a political ideal as it diverts women from the power and honour of an enfleshed sexually alive femaleness that is more natural than its thin counterpart. Wolf goes further: she asserts that culture gives women only two ideals, the pornographic and the anorexic, and the anorexic is sexually safer.[15] Neither of these ideals of course is based in who women really are. They are simply models that fit the current form of patriarchy under which we live. Wolf insists, 'As women we must claim anorexia as political damage done to us by a social order that considers our destruction insignificant because of what we are – less.'[16] Of course Wolf is aware that throughout much of human history the fat female body has not received the treatment it now receives and she has a suggestion: the cultural obsession with thinness, she says, is not about beauty – it is about obedience.[17]. No surprise then that the fat female body is attacked at a time when women want more space in terms of equality. It stands to reason that the female body will be required to shrink publicly when there is a cultural memory of large female bodies as strong and powerful. In the present climate of equality that would be too much for patriarchy to stand!

Wolf and others have given us a place to stand to examine the values, the politics, behind the size debates. Instead of being satisfied with a shallow analysis that states fat people have no willpower or no pride in themselves, we are able to ask questions about the value placed on thinness and to expose those values. What do they say about the society in which we live? In a society where many perfectly healthy women are modelling themselves on an anorexic ideal we have to ask if there is something in our society that worships death. As a Christian society we certainly have a central symbolic put in place over two thousand years that values death and the suffering that precedes it as a redemptive act, one that profoundly changes things and gives meaning and eternal happiness. As we shall see later, the redemptive narrative is not unknown in slimming clubs. Of course we also have a profound dualism that devalues the body and gives immense importance to things above and beyond the body. Along with this we have rhetoric about interiors being more important than exteriors and so, in some perverse way, are we giving importance to a sign of beauty that actually values the stripping away of exteriors? I can not help but wonder in this technological world in which we live if women are also being pressurised to become the automatons that we seem to prize so highly. I would of course not be the first to think this – the Stepford Wives are a classic example of this almost unthinkable scenario. However, with more and more young girls and women walking around in the half-minded daze of anorexia, disconnected and half awake, we are perhaps not as far from that reality as we may have hoped.

God, the hard upright male?

It is of course entirely possible given our Christian heritage that we are not simply terrified of bodies but particularly so of soft bodies, bodies that come over the edges a little. These bodies not only make us appear soft and yielding – they also seem a little vulnerable, not hard and defended by muscle and chiselled lines. The lean body looks controlled and repressed, it looks ready to repel invasion and to resist temptation – in this secular world it is surprising that we have here a classic biblical God imaged in human flesh. James Nelson has shown us how the phallic god invades Christian thinking: this is the hard, big and up god that Nelson believes has been fashioned from some pre-Christian thinking and some dualistic metaphysics.[18] Nelson argues that the image of a Christian god that has no need of anything and no vulnerability has been prevalent despite the central symbolic of incarnation and crucifixion, and it is from this image of a god without need that phallocentric theology has emerged. God becomes the phallus in the sky, the one who is no-relational, self-sufficient, powerful and, in short, hard. Of course once this god is projected into the sky he works his way back to earth and influences what we understand as acceptable humanness. Nelson has demonstrated exceptionally well how this model affects male sexuality and spirituality; he asks men to be more realistic, to create a theology as much based in the penis, the soft and wrinkled everyday reality, as it is in the hard and up, always right, penetration model of the divine. In short, he is asking men to think in terms of the soft god and he demonstrates how this will affect their relationship in a positive way. He understands that he is up against generations of tradition that have seen softness as femaleness and by association down the centuries not as close to God.

While his work has been mainly in the area of male sexuality and relationship I think Nelson gives us an insight into the hard god that lurks in Christianity and the way in which that god has influenced sexuality and spirituality, both of which I think lurk in the depths of the contemporary fat/lean debates. We have over the centuries developed a culture that represses flesh and now we see that a culture has emerged, like no other time in history, which eroticises the bare bones of women. In this age that views itself as totally secular, more secular than ever before, we have a female ideal that would please many of the Church Fathers – what an irony and what psychological questions this raises, but that is for another author! The female body is reduced to a flat surface devoid of warmth, tenderness and mystery and 'our erotic ideal has become as hard and unyielding perhaps as the love relationships that dominate social life'.[19] As a theologian I am fascinated by the prospect that the phallic god may have broken loose and be influencing secular society in a dangerous way, that is to say, the detachment that he was expected to feel may have taken total hold of our hearts too – and in his absence we are embodying his ideals through the hard, controlled body ideals that we expect from women. This is a dangerous god as Nelson has demonstrated, and so one that needs rebellion in the form of fleshy women, women whom the Goddess would delight in! This is a rebellion for hearts as well as minds and bodies, it is a rebellion that calls for a softer world, a more embracing and yielding world, a vulnerable yet powerful world – a world in which edges are permeable and incarnation becomes more complete.

Sadly we are not there yet and women still live out the controlling god through the illusion that dieting demonstrates control in their world and that somehow it makes them appear better people. The reality is that many women are trapped in the image that has been projected onto the vast consumer screen of their lives and so are not in control at all. They are condemned to feelings of shame and failure rather than power and empowerment and perhaps even to illness and maybe death in the pursuit of a reality that is not theirs. Research in the USA shows that two-thirds of women are on diets and spend approximately $7 billion on weight-loss products that either do not work or have very damaging side effects. The tragedy of all this is that these women are generally not overweight but rather are giving in to the perception that any flesh on a female is morally bad. In so doing they place themselves at risk of illness and they do not gain the power they assume they will. How could they, given that they have played the game by rules set out by the male gaze? This is a no-win situation, but women are so disconnected from their own desires that it is often hard for them to realise the dangerous game they are playing. (The question of female desire will be looked at in a later chapter.)

Just too much flesh

As we shall see as we progress, the issues of food, sex and female desire are linked in many ways. The most extreme cultural expressions of the fear of women who are seen as 'too much', usually in relation to sexuality, are interestingly often expressed through eating and hunger metaphors – the frightening all-consuming woman, the one to be controlled. In films we often find that women showing unrestrained delight in eating operates as sexual foreplay. In commercials where the food is an erotic experience women are only allowed so much but what they have is highly sexually charged. This is not a new phenomenon. The Victorians were very rigid about what a woman could eat and whether she should eat it in public as the pleasure might be too much to be seen in the public domain. Women were warned against too much stimulation from food, and books were written to show the desirable and undesirable affects of certain foods – some were suitable for women and others for men only. As always with the Victorians, there was another side and this was more salacious. For them the fat body was excessive, exotic, sensual sex outside the normal. So when fat was enticing it was something out of bounds, exciting for its marginality.[20] This discourse was ringed around with language of the Fall and eating, and of course the issue of the control of women was central to it since Eve and an apple figure so significantly in the story of the Fall. No wonder Marx tells us that the body is not an ideological reality alone, but a cultural and economic reality, and everything depends on what body you have and where it sits in the power structure.

Despite the cultural representations of women as insatiable over both food and sex, there is another picture emerging, one that is the opposite of what we are told and profoundly disturbing. Research that is now emerging suggests that there is a very real link between bulimia, anorexia and sexual abuse. Male psychologists and psychiatrists have been slow to accept these findings, and ten years after female clinicians have reported significant correlations there is still doubt and scepticism. The main problem is the way in which histories are reported, but there may also be a male reluctance to see male roles in female illness.[21] Further, of course, we forget that the idea of non-consensual sex between an adult male and a woman or child has until recently been endorsed by the law – rape in marriage was made illegal only very recently and the age for girls to marry was twelve at the beginning of the last century in the UK and remained at this age in many of the states in the USA until much more recently. So we are still caught in a conceptual world that lies between two rather different realities and is struggling to find new articulations. This is further complicated by the strange world in which we find ourselves where men claim to prefer women who are childlike and dependent with less than full mature female bodies. In such a world it is not surprising that our children get used as though they were adult women. I do not have space to go into the question of the relationship between abuse and eating disorders here but I mention it as the research does appear to show that abuse affects the neurotransmitters that influence eating – one in four women are abused and one in five women have eating disorders. What are we to make of this?

Rita Brock[22] would find that it yelled about the lack of relationality and vulnerability that we have in society and she would see it as calling for healing, the kind of healing that she feels as central to the Christian life. This is not the kind of healing that comes from the laying on of hands. Rather, incarnation demands that justice is lived in and through the body. In a real sense it demands that the bodies of women and men be free from oppression and are able to flourish. Our political action is then as curative as any laying on of hands. Indeed, it is community action that aids growth in mutuality, unlike 'dispensed healing', which disempowers us and makes us mere spectators in our own lives. Brock powerfully writes:

> Heart is our original grace. In exploring the depths of heart we find incarnate in ourselves the divine reality of connection, of love ... But its strength lies in fragility. To be born so open to the presence of others in the world gives us the enormous, creative capacity to make life whole. Yet such openness means that the terrifying and destructive factors of life are also taken into the self, a self that then requires loving presence to be restored to grace.[23]

Millions of women are affected by eating disorders of various kinds and few women are comfortable with food, eating and size. This is a real sickness. It seems the cause is abuse be it sexual or otherwise, that is to say the abuse of attacking a person in their body with preconceived ideas and ideals and reinforcing this through cultural actions and requirements. As a theologian I see this as a blasphemy, a blasphemy against the divine/human reality that incarnation declares and therefore an issue that requires theological healing too. It seems to me that Brock may have a way for this problem to be addressed which is as political as it is spiritual. If incarnation is to flourish then we have to flourish in our bodies, not simply in some disembodied part of ourselves – it is attention to this part alone that has caused many problems as we have seen through the centuries – but in the fullness of what it is to be human, freed from the false projections and aspirations of control. Understanding healing as she does, Brock gives us a way to approach the complex question of women and their bodies under patriarchy that moves us beyond the models of individual weakness or sickness and places the issue in the public sphere where action may be taken to overcome the patriarchal roots of women's discomfort in their bodies. As we will see later, I believe Brock's understanding dovetails very well with erotic and empowering Christology, which I will be suggesting is the way for empowerment for women. For now I wish to note that she offers us political will and possibilities in an area traditionally seen as simply signalling yet another place of weakness where the 'not good enough' woman lives.

The secular feminists who have been mentioned so far have been suggesting that this whole issue is political and so they call for political action to resist it. What is encouraging as a theologian is that while we may see the roots of the problem as perhaps theological in origin it has also become possible to see some areas of resistance as having a theological base too. Weightism is not based in undeniable medical or psychological facts – the fat will not all drop dead, cost the NHS millions or be psychological cases – so it is a prejudice which assumes things about personality, morality, intelligence, relational life and ultimately worth, and as such has to be challenged. There is a huge exaggeration about the dangers of the flesh as there was in the rhetoric about the dangers of female sexuality, and it seems that this almost 'fire and brimstone' anti-fat rhetoric is also based in body hatred and distrust. We can but wonder why we seem to have developed a morality of orality, one in which women are seen as out of control if they open their mouths.[24] This of course is not new in Christianity, where women's silence has been encouraged. As we see, women and food/eating is a language of its own, a speaking out, and so as such will also need to be policed and inhibited. As sexuality was before it, eating and orality is a matter of power and control: the power lies with those who appear to be outside the discourse gazing in with what they claim is a dispassionate and objective gaze, but in reality it is the gaze of the powerful, of those who are not gazed at but those who control. Just as we have seen with sexuality,[25] so now with food, girls police their own desires in the light of the male gaze and in so doing become disempowered. Research has shown that eating disorders such as bulimia are disorders of denial, disconnection and disempowerment, and so recovery is about empowerment and speaking the truth about desire. As I have shown in much of my earlier work, for women to speak their desire is no easy matter – we do not in most cases have the language, let alone the safe space in which to find the words and reconnect with the body that is the basis of that desire. How difficult it still is for us to know what is normal for us in a society that denies female desire at every turn, that is, we see it portrayed everywhere but it is what men wish to see, not necessarily what women wish to express. We still operate in a patriarchal frame where it is the weakness of women that is considered to be the most feminine characteristic, and it is perhaps not a large step to see that the encouragement of eating disorders through cultural stereotypes that make that weakness tangible would not be understood as a crime against humanity, although that is in reality what it is. Such a crime is indeed political, yet making this case in these apolitical days when it is commonly held that we are all free is a hard task indeed and one that runs the risk of being understood as a Neolithic feminist rant!

Perhaps there is a chance of making the case when we consider that anorexia was first spotted as a phenomenon, rather than as the occasional individual case, amongst white upper- and middle-class women who were, through their educational opportunities, competing for what had traditionally been male jobs. It is more than curious that there was this outbreak amongst those who were looking for equality and recognition; they learnt that despite education and capability they always remained women, the object of the male gaze, and as such they needed to take this along with their minds to the boardroom. The lesson was a harsh one – equality is always the gift of the powerful and as such is no reality at all.

There is a strange double bind here too: while women are food for the male gaze they also feel under pressure to undervalue child care and nurture. Some would say this is the fault of the feminist movement which encouraged women into the workplace as never before. Of course this was true, but it was also true that, as Audre Lorde reminds us, the master's tools will never dismantle the master's house. So there was a call for the business world that these women entered to be radically changed. Some things have changed but we are far from a feminist utopia and it may also be said that the corporate world has to some degree tainted the feminist soul! However, the result of the devaluing of the female nurturer also seemed to mean that the female body in the male workplace should resemble that world through the body, so the curves were replaced by the lean, muscular bodies honed in the corporate gyms. Once again the female was dis-empowered. Susan Bordo[26] claims that the curves of the sex goddess such as Sophia Loren were politically expedient in that they were physical representations of what a woman was meant to do – serve the man, the home, the family. She was the nurturer in the house and as such needed the soft yielding welcoming and comforting body. Bordo suggests that the lean body stripped of any maternal qualities is the one desired by men in the male world because it does not offer any alternative female values, but blends in with the existing male hierarchy so that there is no symbolic competition. She claims that the obese in our society are the targets of such blinding rage and disgust, not for size alone but for symbolic representation, a representation of alternatives and challenges.

What large bodies challenge in the heart of patriarchy is an interesting question to ponder. What are they refusing to be normalised into? This is a question to keep before us as we continue the investigation, and it will be taken up later in the book, but at first glance it appears that the fat body carries with it the power of the matriarch and all that she represents on the cultural symbolic landscape as well as the psychic one. We do after all come into the world between the fleshy thighs of a woman – is this where all the trouble starts? Women as well as men are not immune from this powerful world of overpowering female flesh, but they react quite differently, as we shall see in Chapter 5. However, it appears to be the case that girls go through the process of becoming women in cultures that do not value women and that also seem to despise female flesh itself.

Kim Chernin[27] believes there is a direct correlation between the standards set for women's beauty and the desire to control and limit the development of women. She demonstrates this through a survey of the last forty years and the rise of feminist consciousness and the equal rights agenda. Starting at 1960 she reminds us that Marilyn Monroe, all size 16 of her, was the icon of female beauty. This was the decade in which women protested against the Miss World beauty competition where women paraded and were judged by the passive male gaze. It was also the same decade in which anorexia as we know it emerged and spread very rapidly amongst those who wished to work in what had been male preserves. In the 1970s bulimia began to be noticed and Weight Watchers opened its doors (it had of course been preceded by diet Workshops as early as 1965). In the mid 1970s the 'addict' status of being overweight was confirmed through the opening of Overeaters Anonymous, which sits well with the psychopathological view of women and weight that was prevalent at that time. Chernin notes that these two very different movements which were competing for the minds and hearts of women, the Women's Movement and the diet industry, had very different languages for women, which she believes highlight social concerns beyond the body.[28] The diet industry spoke of shrinking, contracting, losing, loss, lessening and lightweightness in relation to women and their bodies. The Women's Movement spoke of large, abundant, powerful, expansive, development, growth, acquiring weight, acquiring gravity and creating wider frames in relation to the lives of women. Interestingly women who embraced either of these options were doing so in order to make sense of the world they inhabited, yet the bodily permissions for them could not have been more different. While those entering the Women's Movement were aware that they entered a political struggle, those who joined diet groups had no idea that this was what they also were doing, as they entered the domain of the body that was highly symbolically charged, and understood the body as something to be shaped according to the political ideals of wider society. Of course this makes it appear that the worlds were divided along very clear lines, but the truth may be nearer to a contradiction in the minds of most women. In truth most women are committed to the idea of their own growth and development, while many are also concerned with the notion of full participation in society, whether they are feminists or not, and at the same time our bodies find it all too easy to be obedient to the conventional world, feminist and non-feminist alike. Chernin's focus on the emergence of the diet industry alongside the Women's Movement is very reminiscent of Mary Daly's[29] claim that the worst excesses of gynaecology emerged at the time of First Wave Feminism. That too was a rhetoric of what would be best for women, how the real woman should be, and a wider rhetoric about health concerns and so on. We would do well not to forget that the removal of the clitoris was medical practice in

Britain until 1947, the reasons being to calm women down, to make them less feisty and to rein in their aspirations to have a place in the public domain. Of course I am not suggesting that this was widely used; there were enough women in the world who did not suffer that fate to demonstrate that its use was limited, but that it existed at all as a possibility and for the reasons given is something to think about from the point of view of body politics. The parallels between what Daly and Chernin suggest are striking – in both cases women have their bodies cut, shaped and reduced. For those with eyes to see this is no hidden political agenda, although in truth it probably does develop under the weight of much unconscious but deep-seated anxiety about women's bodies.

Our culture still does not embrace the idea of whole and empowered women, and so the stress and contradictory pressure on women is immense. This may help to explain why in an era of feminism we see an abundance of overweight women alongside emaciated bodies. This signals to me that the underlying questions to do with women and bodies have not been addressed even by secular feminism and its invaluable contribution to the body politic. As a theologian I wish to suggest that some of the roots of the problem are buried in Christian dualism and the way in which men in their efforts to escape the realities of their own bodies have projected the 'problems' of embodiment on to women. The female body has always signalled much more of the reality of life. The birth and death cycles are clearer on the female body and, as we shall see, men have hidden from this through theological constructions that attempt to tell a different story. The female body has in most parts of history paid a heavy price to protect men from some harsh truths. Under Christianity, when the body was no longer viewed as the mirror of divine perfection but rather as an enslaver and source of humiliation, the burden on female flesh became greater, as we shall see in the next chapter. Christianity added another interesting part to the body equation, the unchanging God as the absolute; this meant that anything that changed, that was flexible and in flux, was far away from God. We are very familiar with how this affected the sexual bodies of women: menstruation, childbirth, menopause all served to demonstrate to the Fathers and beyond that the female body was unstable and not made in the image of the unchanging God. However, when we move the discourse to that of size we see some interesting points of connection. A body that can fluctuate in size – as all bodies can but women's do quite regularly pre-menstruation, while pregnant and after menopause – demon-strates the kind of dynamic embodiment that has always been worrying within fixed theological circles. This deeply rooted notion of the unchanging God may be argued to be at work today under a secular guise. Foucault has demonstrated how the power of the 'norm' emerged at the end of the eighteenth century and with it a discourse about the universally applicable standards expected of the human body; he shows how these bodies and those who lived in them became ranked according to their differ-entiation from an unattainable ideal and how this ranking fed into a social hierarchy. This of course had very practical con-sequences, with insurance companies developing height and weight charts which further standardised individuals and also exerted power in their lives. Those who fell outside the charts literally paid the price either with higher premiums or no pre-miums at all. The norm was of course static, so what also devel-oped was a control system to maintain the norm. Foucault argues that this was in itself a pervasive form of social coercion.[30] This desire for normalisation was much more than a health concern alone since the insurance charts were created in an almost random way, so that the complexity of bodies and society become apparent in the area of weight as they have in the area of sexu-ality. The theologian in me wonders if such an emphasis on the static notion of the norm could ever have developed from a Goddess culture where the strength and divine nature of the Goddess is precisely demonstrated by her ability to change and to manifest in a glorious array of diverse beauty. No surprise really that what Foucault is demonstrating as an eighteenth-century manifestation of social coercion can, with very little mental gymnastics, be seen as another outbreak of God the almighty and unchanging absolute. In my view we do well to keep before us the Christian heritage of the West if we are ever fully to understand and overcome even contemporary forms of oppression and coercion.

Fat girls, Christianity and society

Christianity has for centuries told us that the good girl keeps her appetite for food, sex and power well under control, while feminist theology has allowed us to think again about this diminishing role. What then are we fat girls identifying as problems within patriarchy? Susie Orbach many years ago reminded us that fat is a feminist issue[31] just as much as anorexia and bulimia. Just like bulimia and anorexia, Orbach understands fat as an enraged response to the inequalities of the sexes and an assertion of strength.[32] While she agrees with the general feminist argument that becoming fat is a way to break free of sexual stereotypes, she also notes that compulsive eating is something that women and not men do, and so must have something to do with the uniqueness of female experience that is beyond the positive embrace of a large body. Orbach is clear that being fat is one way to subvert the male gaze and to attempt to achieve some kind of subjectivity rather than understanding oneself as an object; a way to look at oneself from the inside rather than policing oneself through the external gaze of self and others. However, she also sees it as rejecting other stereotyped roles, such as the ever-giving nurturer, the mother who is meant to feed and to be the last to feed. Orbach claims that the fat body rejects that self-sacrificial role for women and replaces it with a body that begins to understand its own needs and the equal importance of those within patriarchal society. This is of course at odds with other theorists who see the round body as the eternal nurturer of others. Orbach highlights how girls are breastfed less than boys and their feeding as children is carried out over shorter periods of time – 50 per cent less time is given to it, since there is a perception that they need less. This leads to less attentive feeding, which she thinks is in itself a feminist issue, preparing women to be the givers and not the takers, but which may also lay the foundations for women to rebel against this shortage in later life. Of course we all come into the world looking for the breast since this is life itself, and here is the rub: what may appear to be just food is also a desire to embrace life and to take hold of the power of that life; so food is our initiator into a world beyond it. At the breast it is our introduction to sensual pleasure and, if that is inhibited for girls, it may well have some effects in later life. It also signals our inclusion and exclusion and our transition beyond boundaries. We are aware that our earliest experiences affect us, and what is more foundational than the way in which we are succoured? This literal act of sustaining our lives signals how worthy that life is within a wider context. It is from this initial sense of worth that we will move through the other boundaries of life. In short, feeling worthy of full inclusion or having a sense of limited worth and so limited access to life's fullness is largely determined at the breast. We have seen how central the act of eating is to the human community and how it does indeed signal status, value and inclusion in the world in which we live.

All this is true for the infant as for the adult, so it is interesting to note that even the apparently natural activity of feeding one's child is highly gendered and lays the foundations of life beyond the breast. For Orbach, then, fat women put a crack in popular culture's ability to make women mere products, from the gaze to the frantic purchasing of the right clothes, make-up and food to maintain the image. This crack is made deeper by what she also believes is a fat woman's rejection of the kind of power and competitiveness that is encouraged by patriarchy between women and beyond into society. Fat women, she argues, take a step back from this kind of maelstrom and decide to be different and to assert their worthiness in other less hierarchical ways. She is also aware that fat women may not wish to exert the kind of power or enter the kind of competitiveness that heteropatriarchy encourages between women in the arena of size. However, Orbach also believes there is another side to the argument which is about women satisfying their own needs and thus declaring adult status for themselves. She is aware that we are not brought up to take care of ourselves in this way and, like other theorists, she sees that adult women are not really what most men want, so the pressure is on to keep denying who we are. To know what and how much we want to eat is not an easy matter in a patriarchal society. Orbach is therefore mindful that many women may fear being thin just as others fear being fat, and it is this line between the two that polices so much of our activity and takes so much of our valuable energy.

Feminists have for generations now being calling for women to begin their recovery from patriarchy through recognition of the ways in which the oppression works. It is, however, relatively recently that the issue of size has been placed within that frame and links made with other forms of patriarchal oppression. Knowing that the personal is political on a wide screen has led some thinkers to understand the links between the control and diminishment of the female body and that of the planet. Certainly under the Christian ideology women and nature have always been linked in a rather downward spiral. The hierarchical dualism that is central to the Christian world-view has placed that which it considers to be more base and fleshy together at the bottom of the pile, and it is here that women and nature have historically battled for survival. Catherine Steiner-Adair[33] sees strong parallels between the struggles of the female body and the struggles of the planet. Both are plagued by tales of starvation, extinction, waste of natural resources, rape and toxic dumping.[34] She demonstrates how anorexics particularly are attempting to make extinct any female features, while supermodels and those who would aspire to emulate them starve and then have their bodies enhanced through the introduction of silicone and other potentially harmful toxic substances. There is the same disrespectful language used about women and the earth, and both are expected to continue to nurture in the face of extreme abuse. She draws further parallels between the disrespect for the natural cycles of life and the cycles of women's bodies, all of which are problematised within a patriarchal system. Weightism encourages women to disassociate themselves from their bodies and even to dismember themselves through various surgical interventions and in so doing, Steiner-Adair argues, women are ripped from their bodies as sources of wisdom, spirituality and power. In the same way, by asserting control over nature and bringing about the destruction of a thousand species a day we are also removing ourselves from empowerment and spiritual wisdom and placing ourselves in a false realm of disassociation. Steiner-Adair puts it this way: 'If we practice a politic based on dominance, separation and autonomy then it is difficult to have a vision of the future in which we nourish and sustain the whole.'[35] Women around the world understand that the negative relation between themselves and nature can be overturned and understood as a positive relationship; perhaps reflecting on the parallels that are suggested here may help even further so that the call for food for the many starving can be heeded. There is enough food to go around yet ten thousand people die every day from starvation while in the western world there is a wilful restriction of food intake – we must begin to see the connections.

I hope this chapter has illustrated that the body can not escape the imprint of culture and gendered interpretations either through external scrutiny or internal censure. There is no view of ourselves from 'nowhere': each way we look carries with it a set of assumptions and preconceptions and in the world in which we currently live those are patriarchal. I do not deny that such views carry a cost for men too, but for women the price is often deadly as we have seen in relation to eating disorders. I hope that as the book progresses theology will enable us to start from the fat body as one that feels no need for excuses and no sense of shame and failure – in short that we can develop a fat liberation theology. Why? Because it will give a voice to those who have been 'invented' through the words, actions and expectations of others for too long, and challenge the preconceptions that affect the lives of millions. I think what has also emerged through this chapter in a way that surprises me is the inequalities of the rhetoric about body shape and size and the way in which individualism has taken hold to such an extent that the body emerges as a vehicle for identity in which we see 'a construction of life as plastic possibility and weightless choice, undetermined by history, social location or even individual biography'.[36] This surprises me as it seems very close to the metaphysical picture that any of the Church Fathers could have painted, yet we live in a secular world, a world in which the body is given so much attention and importance – yet it still seems to be a body that is not really there. We are still confronted with make-believe bodies, bodies that have no true value in themselves but carry a great deal of cultural and moral meaning. As an incarnational theologian I am concerned because it is in and through the flesh that what we understand as redemptive praxis takes place – if we are so alienated from our bodies then we are unable to live the fullness of incarnation. What appears to be emerging is what may be called secular metaphysics and like so many things it is almost undetectable, yet it is dangerous. Christian metaphysics has not allowed us to live in our skins and has led to many kinds of alienation within and between us which have inhibited the full becoming of women and men through the creation of false and destructive dualisms. Theology has helped us to see this – can we now see that same thing at work yet unnamed within the secular world? As a liberation theologian I have a materialist, historical approach to creative/redemptive action and so I am always concerned when I come across rhetoric that appears to place us in some ahistorical space. What has been shown in this chapter is that the discourses about female bodies and size have come from that place and have invaded the psyche to such an extent that women even believe that their salvation from their unruly and slightly threatening bodies also lies in that place. As we have seen, the boundary between fat and thin is a very anxious one for women and so is the ideal place where they can be drawn into distrust of their bodies and the power relations that society wishes to impose. Of course as Butler[37] tells us, this marginal area is also the weak spot of any power system. It has to be highly policed to maintain it, and while it is therefore a place of great stress for people who have to be kept in line it is also vulnerable to rebellion and breakthrough. Women who do not fit the anorexic model, finding the inner strength to declare that we are beautifully and awesomely made, may just crack and crumble one pillar of patriarchy and free us to embrace more of our divine/human fullness. As we shall see in the next chapter, this has not always been possible for women over the last two thousand years under patriarchal Christianity.[38]

Chapter Two

The gate is narrow: creating theological body boundaries

The beginning and end of all God's work is embodiment.[1]

As we have had demonstrated many times the question of women and embodiment has been a problem for Christianity; a religion that declared incarnation as salvific has never sat too well with the realities of living beings, particularly women. Much attention has been given to women and sexuality and much less to women and food within the Christian tradition, although as we shall see some work has been done on this. The time seems right to look at this is some detail since the secular world, so renowned for living out in blissful oblivion so much of its sup- posedly rejected Christian heritage, is becoming very despising of large bodies in a way that would make the Church Fathers proud. In addition it is also praising the almost invisible female body, understanding this as a sign of great success and moral standing. As the chapter progresses we will see that this is not an unfamiliar pattern in the worst excesses of ascetic Christian piety aimed at women and in some cases voluntarily taken up by women.

Organic eating from Eden

So what does the Christian tradition have to offer us as resources for navigating our way through the pressing questions concerned with women, food and size? The early Christian readers of Genesis saw the first act of disobedience and thus the Fall of Man as based in food and eating. In this action Eve took the lead and Adam followed, but it was the curiosity and appetite of the woman that brought the man to his ruin. This led to many of the early thinkers of the Church having harsh words to say about food: Basil of Caesarea believed that gluttony brought death to Adam and wickedness to the world through the 'lust of the belly'.[2] It was, then, the pleasure of taste that drove us from Paradise and these pleasures are seen as akin to sexual pleasure. Tertullian thought the genitals were close to the stomach to show us that gluttony and lust are linked, while Clement of Alexandria believed we had to keep tight control of the stomach and the organs beneath it.[3] This was not entirely new thinking as much of the ancient world also understood there to be a connection between food and lust, so when Jerome declared that it was eating that turned the hitherto non-sexual Adam and Eve into sexual practitioners very few people were surprised. It also followed that if chastity could lead us back to the original pre-lapsarian paradise then food must also be linked with that process. Augustine was suspicious of chillies, believing they inflamed the passions and thus led us from our divine destiny – strangely he may have been right, as today's food gurus tell us that hot spicy food can be rather sexy. Chastity, so necessary for salvation, was linked with culinary habits also and sin could be just one morsel away.

The Desert Fathers believed they fasted to make amends for the sin of Adam, that is, eating, and their theology was shaped by the notion of conquering temptation that attacked them in their stomachs and their loins. There were also ideas about what it was all right to eat and as with much Christian theology this rested on declarations about what they must have eaten in Eden. Tertullian believed that the first pair was vegetarian, while Jerome thought that Christians who gave up meat and wine could recapture something of that innocence of Eden. This is extraordinary theology when we consider that Christ, in their understanding, was meant to have moved us beyond all the superficial matters such as food. It just shows how closely they believed food and sex to be linked since as we know they were never able to come to terms with sexuality in a satisfactory and creative way.

There is another interesting point to ponder in the Genesis story: humans are said to be made from the very stuff they then have to toil over to provide food.[4] The link between the two is very deep indeed and Stone wonders if there are ancient echoes of the Gilgamesh Epic here, which understands that animals only become human when they have eaten and drunk – when their connection with the earth is established at that very basic level.[5] As a Christian theologian I wonder if that 'becoming' of humans that seems linked with food gets further extended in the metaphors to do with the Bread of Life, through which it could be argued a further metamorphosis takes place from human to divine. Perhaps I am arguing that when we get to the core of who we are, enfleshed, living and breathing persons with appetites, then we begin to understand who we really are, divine/human incarnations with appetites of all kinds and deep connection with the earth that bore us.

Stone reminds us that eating in the Hebrew Bible is not all bad even when interpreted through the dualist minds of the Fathers. The Israelites are brought to the land of milk and honey and as long as they obey God they will have their fill: here we see that being satisfied is not all about sin, it can be about the reward of God for good living (Deuteronomy 11:8–17). Abundance and eating well can then also be seen as part of salvation as indeed it is in the notion of the Messianic Banquet, the utopia where all are fed and all sit at the same table to eat their fill. However, as we shall see, this may be an ideal image for after death or the end times, but it has not always been matched in theological thought and spiritual discipline before death, both of which have been rather ascetic in outlook and praxis. Stone[6] draws our attention to the connection between the word of God and food in the Hebrew Bible: both Ezekiel and Jeremiah speak of eating the word of God, ingesting the scroll in the case of Ezekiel (3:3) and declaring it to be as sweet as honey. This very intimate and consuming relation between the word of God and the person is worth pondering. In our world, every day tens of thousands, including 31,000 children, die from lack of food, it is estimated that 828 million people are suffering from hunger, and many hundreds are dying from the effects of a long-term diet of inadequate and unwholesome food, which is all they can afford. In these circumstances we are perhaps being asked to consider the economic and social implications of the word of God tasting like honey. Personally I am not drawn to the idea of making the consecrated host my only food, as many have been. Rather, when pondering this, I am keen to examine the way in which food distribution and the appalling standards of cheap food production take place. For me if the word of God is to be as sweet as honey, then we need to find a way in which the more than adequate resources of the world (there is enough for each person to have a 2,500-calories-a-day intake) are distributed in a healthy way to its inhabitants. Then and only then will food taste sweet, for it will be the nectar of God. The way we deal with food in this advanced capitalist world means that we are not ingesting the relational, mutual and empowering word of God – rather we are toxic in our thinking and our divisive consuming.

Mary Douglas is amongst those who tells us that food, as well as sex, is usually bound up with religious laws since both help create the boundaries of a society. We see that the Hebrew Bible is full of food counsel and certainly what is ingested and what is forbidden is central to the whole concept of being an Israelite. For anthropologists like Douglas there is nothing surprising in this since the human body symbolises the larger social body and so has to be moulded to form the group identity. The reason that food and sex are so well organised and policed is because the orifices are the vulnerable points of the body and so by extension are the edges of the discourse about the body social. So we see that Judith Butler may be right in the assertion that the edges of any discourse are excellent points for resistance.[7] They are most heavily policed since they are most easily subverted, and they are the outer edges of social identity. Stone puts it this way: 'As eating and sexual intercourse involve the transgression of the body's boundaries and the incorporation by the body of foreign substances food and sex function as powerful symbolic markers of the boundaries between social units.'[8] Food often acts as a marker between people both ethnically and socially; we are all aware of the racial prejudices that are carried through speaking of food and certainly any walk through a supermarket will alert one to economic and social differences. How is it that we know that from a food trolley? Of course there are also gendered implications in our food divisions and prohibitions beyond those fostered through personal 'choice'. Religious ritual, as well as top chefs, also place great store on the way in which food is prepared, who may touch it and when, and who may ingest it. We are also aware of how people may place themselves on the social hierarchy through an ability to distinguish authentic exotic food from the westernised version – this gives an air of sophistication that was once simply associated with wine discernment! In short, then, there is a hierarchy in food that has its origins in the religious traditions that serve to distinguish one ethnic or cultural group from another. Food, just like sex, has always been a way to distinguish the 'other' and it is interesting to me that Protestant Christianity with its low emphasis on the sharing of eucharistic food has been the very religion to develop the 'Slim For Him' programme, which I will concentrate on in the next chapter, which most certainly identifies the in and the out group on the grounds of food ingestion and size. Perhaps I should not be at all surprised, and if I take my lead from anthropologists then it is possible to see just why this might be, but more of that later.

Eat, drink; be drunk with love

Turning once more to the Hebrew Bible, with the help of Stone we see that food was also used as a sign of hospitality, of accepting others beyond the boundaries, of sharing who we are as well as the food we make. Abraham (Genesis 18) is hospitable to strangers through the sharing of food, and indeed much Near Eastern hospitality involves the sharing of food. This biblical notion helps us understand in a new way the prohibition of the Church Fathers of gluttony, which becomes far less a sin of excess than of not welcoming, of being so focused on one's own needs as to ignore the needs of others. In a strange way then we may accuse the 'Slim For Him' gang of gluttony as they are obsessed with their own needs in this ever decreasing circle of self-absorption. There is little doubt that in the Hebrew Bible eating involved holiness and the dietary laws all aimed at creating the correct relationships between people. Interesting for Christians then that Jesus, coming from this background, fed people. Shannon Jung argues that the Jewish feasts were occasions for the whole body of people to renew their covenant promises to God and that in, for example, Isaiah 25:6–9 we see the ultimate eschatological banquet, the time in which deliverance and restoration all occur, happening when people feast together.[9] Of course this banquet notion is also carried on in the Christian scriptures and we see through the gospels that all kinds of outcasts are invited to the table, thus showing that hospitality overtakes any exclusion. Food does indeed become one of those unstable edges that Douglas and Butler both talk about; in the Christian story it becomes an edge that allows all to come in – that is the theory anyway.

Stone reminds us that in the Song of Songs two of the potentially disruptive edges are mentioned together, sex and food. The way in which they are used in this text offers very real alternatives to women under patriarchy, but of course just as there are alternatives offered so are there dangers in this potential. When I have written about this before it has been in the context of sexual revolution for women but it also remains true that there are pleasures and dangers in food for women too, particularly in a patriarchal society that demands certain shapes to please the male gaze. In the Song of Songs right from the beginning of the text the woman is asserting that her lover's love is better than wine and his fruit is sweet in her mouth (2:3). His joy is also evident in the text when he declares her genitals are 'an orchard of pomegranates with excellent fruit' (4:13). The orality of these passages and the constant emphasis on fruit are both significant when we look to this text for a challenge to the dualistic patriarchal interpretations of sexuality. The Christian tradition has used this text to underpin its dualistic and hierarchical rhetoric about the sustaining power of the mystical marriage as opposed to the fleeting and shallow pleasures of sexual love. Here, with an emphasis on sexual love as food, indeed fruit, we find a real challenge to that rhetoric. Food is life-sustaining and fruit a wonderful riot of juicy taste and texture, a delightful addition to any diet but nonetheless a life-sustaining and preserving addition. By coupling sex and fruit in this text the author is celebrating the life-sustaining aspect of sexuality beyond that of the merely procreative and introducing us to the idea that the more tastes, textures and smells we encounter the richer life is. So the more immersed in sensuality we become the more our lives are enriched and indeed the more we challenge the patriarchal order. For the present purpose we also see that food and desire are the catalysts for moving beyond a patriarchal order; they are the edges, and when coupled with another edge, that of sexuality, the mix is potentially explosive for patriarchal control. The sheer sensual delight of fruit opens up a world that challenges the contained order.

The Near East certainly used agricultural images when referring to sex, but they were highly patriarchal: the seed was planted in the field and the valuable issue came forth. There is none of that in this text, the seed and field are replaced with the ripening, taste and engorgement of fruit, and phallic procreative images are not to be seen.[10] This is an important starting point for any challenge to heteropatriarchy as practised today. The interesting use of fruit in this text places the lovers within a larger circle of creation but also makes it difficult to identify the giver and receiver of pleasure, the mouth being an active receptor in eating. This is an important point as it lifts these texts from the worst excesses of male pornographic fantasy into a more empowering position for the woman and the man. The man is ecstatic in his claims that he has 'come to my garden … I have eaten my honeycomb with my honey, I have drunk my wine with my milk' (5:1). The eating images disrupt phallic notions with 'their frequent demarcation of subjects and objects, known to us from many ancient representations of sexuality'.[11] The clear desire of the woman for oral stimulation is not the epitome of patriarchal phallic sexuality. The woman here is no simple object, she is also a subject of her own desire, she eats and is eaten, she indulges in a riot of taste and smell.

What is very interesting for the purpose of this book is that the sexuality and sensuality expressed through the imagery of food is not only expressed outside the patriarchal order of social control, but also outside what we today see as normal-sized bodies. The woman in this text challenges views about her body expressed by those who would oppose her or control her, she is a very 'body positive' woman. She affirms her black comeliness against the comments of the daughters of Jerusalem and pushes back her brother's comments that she has no breast with an emphatic celebration of their magnificence (8:10). She tells her lover that her body is a bountiful feast which she will give to him – no question for her that he takes it, but rather that she bestows her great beauty and bounty upon him. This bounty includes an abdomen that is a 'round bowl' full of mixed wine, a heap of wheat surrounded by flowers below breasts that are clusters of fruit growing on palm trees and vines. Her own embodiment pleases her and her lips drip nectar at her own beauty. This is a self-confident and body-celebratory woman, and we could do with more like her in the present day when women spend much of their time and resources attempting to reshape and repackage their comeliness. Her celebration of her ethnic origin is also an inspiration in a world where the signifiers of beauty have become largely European or North American. Many women of colour are reshaping eyes, mouths, noses, to conform to the European model, whereas it would be a revolution of some proportions if they declared their pride in the beauty of their embodied selves as this women does.

The text also makes us aware of the dangers that this self-confident and embodied woman faces but nevertheless she should, I believe, be an inspiration for our own embodied revolutions. She is nameless even though she has a voice – is she then 'everywoman'? Are we to name her in our own desire and erotic becoming? Should the cry of this text, 'Eat, friends, drink. Be drunk with love' (5:2), be central to any Christian body theology? I would of course like to argue that this woman and not Eve, who was punished for her appetite, should be the model for Christian womanhood. It would make such a difference in many aspects of women's lives and to the planet itself. There is a significance in this text in the way that the lovers through connection with food make a profound connection with the earth. Their relationship is not in this way insular but is rather placed in the broadest possible context, that of creation itself.

While Stone puts forward a largely positive case for food from the perspective of the Hebrew Bible he also signals some warning signs. While God provides food for the Israelites during the Exodus there are also many warnings that it is only food provided by God that will satisfy, the food offered to Baal and then eaten will not satisfy. The female deities associated with agriculture are also suspect (Jeremiah 44:15–19), while the good woman provides food that is safe since she provides it in the home (Ben Sira 15:1–3). A gendered aspect of the private/public debate enters with this understanding of food, since woman is seen as in the home providing what is safe while what is offered in public may not be safe and holy. Despite the reservations and certain containments, Stone suggests that the Hebrew Bible shows a God who wants us to embrace life in its fullness through grasping joy in the shape of food, wine and sex (Ecclesiastes 9:7–9).[12] This, then, can be argued to be a God of resistance, the God at the edges, who despite the restrictions placed by priests of religion will allow a glimpse of another alternative, the one of hospitality and abundance.

God the protein junkie bodybuilder!

Another interesting avenue to explore if we wish to assess our body/food heritage is that taken by Stephen Moore who asks what God's body may be like? For Moore this is no simple question, but is underpinned by a Foucauldian understanding of power. Moore does not deal directly with the issue of food but his analysis is helpful here as it sets before us a kind of body ideal that Christians perhaps unconsciously, even consciously, hold about God, in whose image they believe themselves to be made. His observation, along with Foucault, that discipline has one purpose, which is to create docile bodies which can then be subjected, used and transformed, is well taken in relation to the regimes of food restriction that have been practised by Christians over the years and that I have argued have seeped into secular society. Moore argues that Christians understood themselves from the beginning to be those who emerged from baptism as bloodless martyrs with no wounds but with heroic obedience etched onto their very being. This obedience does, he argues, resemble the kind of docility that Foucault talks of, the kind that requires a reshaping of the person through a kind of slave mentality. There would appear to be plenty of scriptural – well at least Pauline – texts to support such an argument (1 Corinthians 9:27; 1 Corinthians 7:22; 2 Corinthians 10:5b). This compliance with the in-group identity is carried on in a way that would be familiar to Douglas, when we read that there is an inner sentinel who fills every orifice (Romans 5:5) – or should we say patrols every margin? The Spirit of God is a rigid extension of his power and it penetrates all believers – here we see the phallic god that Nelson speaks about once again filling all the space and making all his own through obedience and discipline.

Moore is an extremely creative theologian and he takes us on a real journey of discovery. Why, we wonder, is this discipline and obedience so important, and how will we look after it? Well, we will resemble the bodybuilder god who lives in the pages of the Bible. Rather a useful suggestion for the main purpose of this book! While we never see God we are told that he eats the meat sacrificed to him from the table of YHWH which is the altar. Moore suggests that this god lives on a high-protein diet[13] and has a perfect physique. He comes to this latter point by some reverse logic, that is to say, Adam is made in the image of God and we have some canonical and extra-canonical testimony about how Adam looked. Ezekiel 28:12 said he had the perfect body; he was indeed the Thalia Golem, the giant who stretched from heaven to earth and from east to west. So splendid was his physique that the angels thought he was God and there is no doubt that this body is male, with the rabbis telling us that Eve was a split in this huge and majestic body.[14] The body of God is a hard penile body and the 'biblical God is the supreme embodiment of hegemonic hypermasculinity'.[15] I wish to argue that it is this hard God who roams in the minds of women ascetics as well as those women who inhabit the business world and feel duty bound to imitate the hard bodies of the men whose jobs they believe they have taken. Of course, this disciplined body does not come from nowhere and Foucault may be right when he says that there is an inner policing in the believer that is so deeply implanted that it becomes indistinguishable from freedom itself. It got there, I wish to argue, almost unconsciously through the hypermasculine body of God that communicates itself not only as acts in the texts but as a sheer presence, one that invades us all. Of course this bodybuilder also becomes through the mediation of his son a superfood himself. Jesus tells us to eat his flesh and drink his blood: 'Whoever eats me will live because of me' (John 6:57), and this alone is the food of everlasting life. The question we need to ask is whether, superfood or not, this is a balanced diet.

Fasting all the way to heaven

Even with this cursory glance we can see that there is a rich and varied heritage for Christians from which to consider the place and significance of food in their spiritual lives and it is to this that I now turn, the ways in which believers have approached the question of food and size. As we may expect, this engagement is as varied as the heritage it builds on. However, a foundational moment is to be found in Eden when the primal pair were believed to have broken the food regulations by ingesting what was prohibited. Aquinas thought that it was the sin of gluttony that brought about the Fall, while Maximus of Turin put it this way: 'What the first man lost by eating the second Adam recovered by fasting. And he kept in the desert the law of abstinence given in Paradise.'[16] Augustine went even further, suggesting that when Christ died he ate us, digested and assimilated us and so made us into a new flesh in his flesh. This is taking the reversal of the Eden events just one step further and indeed placing a great deal of theological significance on the idea of food and eating. We should, it seems, not be surprised, then, to find a return to the events in Eden in one way or another throughout Christian dealings with food, the aim being to put right what went so badly wrong. Fasting was seen as one way to do this and once the practice was established theologies developed around it such as that of Tertullian who believed that an emaciated body was necessary in order to pass through the narrow gate and, further, that only light bodies could be resurrected. In line with Douglas's theories about the edges of bodies we will not be surprised to see that Christians believed that food was susceptible to demonic forces which could inhabit it in order to enter the body. This is why grace was said and food was blessed before being ingested; meat was particularly open to this kind of demonic invasion and so it was limited in some Christian diets. Through the ages many fasting regimes have been developed and have affected different groups, since it has not always been the case that it was expected from all people. For example, in the fourth century a forty-day fast before Easter was developed and later this became also a fast before Christmas and before Pentecost; this increase gathered pace until by the medieval period almost one-third of the church year was taken up with the practice. This was no voluntary activity either, as those who did not join the fast were excluded from church celebrations, and in some cases had their front teeth knocked out or were even killed. Eventually the church had to make concessions for the old, the very young and the infirm and this too spread, so that total abstinence was no longer required. Many readers will be aware that fasting during Lent did not actually mean not eating but rather modifying what one ate, and others will also be familiar with the pre-eucharistic fast that was once required. There was never just one meaning for these fasting activities either; certainly there was often a penitential aspect and an ascetic meaning, but it was also believed that limiting food would help people receive dreams, revelations and visions. In a way that is true, since excessive restriction could lead to hallucinations, although it also has to be acknowledged that present-day anorexics claim that limiting food intake enables them to think more clearly. Much emphasis has been placed on ideas around food consumption and restriction over the Christian centuries and, as we shall see, it still carries a great deal of theology.

There also appears to have been a great deal of competition in fasting: the Desert Fathers seem regularly to up their game if they hear of another monk eating less than they do. Macarius of Alexandria only ate one pound of bread a day and only cabbage leaves on Sunday, while Battheus of Edessa was said to only eat the maggots from his teeth.[17] If this seems extreme then it has to be said that the Irish monks had a reputation for being the most excessive in their fasting. These monks did indeed report that they received visions and that all kinds of miraculous events occurred to them, but it seems that their main motivation for fasting was to subdue the body, particularly the lustful body. As we saw in Chapter 1, this would indeed happen since semi-starvation does lower, if not eliminate, the libido. It also lends itself to some severe mood swings and lack of self-esteem – it seems more than unfortunate, then, that the wisdom of these men has been passed down through the ages to centuries of believers who have attempted to model themselves on this wisdom. They were after all in the grip of extreme personality alteration due to food restriction. By the twelfth and thirteenth centuries more women were taking part in the fasting activities and we begin to see examples of women who claim to live only on the consecrated host. Mary of Oignies could only swallow the host and she claimed she could not even stand the smell of food, while Joan the Meatless had not eaten except for the host for fifteen years. Angela of Foligno, Domenica del Paradisio and Ludwina of Schiedam were just some of the women who claimed not to eat except for the host for periods of time ranging from fifteen to twenty-eight years. Others such as Hedwig of Silesia kept a very strict diet consisting mainly of bread and milk with the occasional small amount of vegetables.

We can be excused for thinking that this excessive approach to food would have been looked on kindly by the church hierarchy, who did indeed seem to approve of it when monks engaged in it. However, this was not always the case and, for example, Catherine of Siena was urged to eat. While she did not eat she gained a great deal of notoriety and was able to take a role in political and religious affairs in a way that was quite unusual for women at the time. She, it has to be remembered, died of starvation! This raises some interesting questions about gender, even though some of the reasoning appears to be genderless. It was felt that rejection of food was in some way rejection of God's creation; this was also to be the approach, many years later, of Zwingli, who saw all things purified by Christ and so all to be appreciated. There were practical concerns such as people becoming too weak to work and so being burdens on their communities, and more spiritual concerns such as rejecting food being regarded as the work of the devil, so that possession was often assumed. The connection between ideas of fasting and demonic possession can be traced back to Babylonian texts, and so has an ancient pedigree. Christians normally thought that this possession could be cured by taking the host or by the intervention of a saint. Many of the famous fasting women such as Catherine of Siena did take food now and again simply to show people they were not possessed. While the devil made some women stop eating he also made others eat, that is to say, there are stories of food temptation associated with the devil – not unlike many adverts today. Maria Magdalen de Pazzi described how the devil threw open cupboards in order to tempt her with the food inside them.[18] It is interesting to note that while many women may have thought, along with Tertullian, that they had to be thin to get through the gates of heaven, the church also thought that women who were light might also be witches since one had to be light to fly. The 'weighing test' became a test for bewitchment, and we hear that the Inquisition often cheated (they once claimed that one woman weighed nothing at all).[19] In order to avoid such a fate women often took themselves to the public witch scale and got a certificate which could be used all across Europe as proof of their non-witch status. These women understood these public weigh-ins as their salvation – now where have we heard that before? There are interesting strands which in themselves do not make a case, but in my eyes do create a frame in which we may understand how women and weight are viewed today. The notion of demonic possession seemed to die down by the seventeenth century, although even in the twentieth century we do have cases of young girls unable to eat being seen as possessed. However, in the case of Annaliese Michel, a young girl who developed paralysis and an inability to swallow, the priest who exorcised her and the parents who allowed it were all had up for neglect in 1975, six years after the phenomenon started. The very idea of neglect signals that it was felt something could and should be done and this is an interesting point to note, since it shows that fasting saints, that had once simply been a problem to the clerical elite and their issues of control, had now become transformed into people with a disorder who could be treated. It would be quite wrong to see this as a move that simply took place in the twentieth century since we do see that public interest in (mainly) women and girls who did not eat was slowly transformed over hundreds of years[20] from a purely spiritual interest, be it in possession or sanctity, to a more 'side show' sort of interest where they were viewed as curious phenomena.

What is of great interest to a feminist theologian is the assertion by the clerical hierarchy of the earlier period that these women who were being such public fasters were acting against humility – not an accusation thrown at the monks – and further that it assumed an authority beyond that of the clerical hierarchy. In other words the fast-er could claim a direct relationship with God which would bypass the clerical elite. Women have throughout church history faced this problem and have dealt with it in a variety of inventive ways. Many of the mystics were accused of going beyond earthly power structure in their relationship with the divine, and most found that speaking humbly about themselves was one way to avoid the flames. It seems, then, that the passive humble female is required within the church and that even while attempting to gain some sense of control in their own lives the women who do so need to be ever mindful that they live within a system that does not value that self-possession within them. It is curious to see that despite encouraging women to eat, the church also handed out severe punishments to those women who claimed they did not eat, yet were found to be doing so – this is a familiar double bind that women find themselves in with food even today.

Holy anorexia or divine ingestion?

It would be almost impossible to suggest that the women we are talking about can be classed as anorexic since that is a culturally bound concept, but we can draw some interesting ideas from understanding the latter while considering the former. Modern day anorexics, we are told, are looking for control in a world they believe does not give them any. Indeed, so sure are they that they have no control that their desire for it does not extend beyond the very edges of their skin: their bodies they can control and so they do. In this way they believe they get a unique identity and one that shows they are in control – after all anorexics are not people without appetites, they are rather people who control their appetites. Just as secular patriarchal society does not expect girls, who are the vast majority of anorexics, to show assertive behaviours, so the church did not expect women to be assertive within it. Rudolf Bell[21] is amongst those who argue that what he calls 'holy anorexia' is closely linked to the hierarchy of the church, which assigned a passive role to its faithful women. The struggle for autonomy, then, is reduced to the limits of the body, just as for the young women in later times, and the authority of the church is sidestepped through this excessive control of the individual body. For Bell these different generations of women do have one thing in common, and that is the fear of losing control. It can be argued that their motivations were very different – the fasting women believed that they would gain union with Christ and they saw the illness that resulted from this rejection of food as just another way to achieve that union. Anorexics, on the other hand, appear to have a fear of being fat, with little philosophical or spiritual influence involved. However, I have argued that we can not draw lines in the sand as easily as that. The spoken influences may appear different, but I do feel there are 'moods and motivations' that pass through the generations and these simply pick up contemporary reasoning to justify the actions. Further, for me the rejection of the passive role, the lack of control, through the regulation of eating speaks loud and clear about the pervasive nature of patriarchy and the price it exacts from the bodies of women through the generations.

Caroline Walker Bynum has made a fascinating study of women and food in the medieval period and she is far less concerned with the psychological aspects of this than Bell appears to be. For her the theological motivation of these women needs to be taken seriously and on its own terms not psychologised through twentieth-century eyes. For medieval Christians food took centre stage in two ways, through fasting and through partaking in the Eucharist. It was also quite common for people to speak of being eaten by God in the way that Augustine[22] did, and so the ingestion process was two-way. Walker Bynum believes that the centrality of food in women's spirituality began to appear in the twelfth and thirteenth centuries in the Low Countries amongst the daughters of wealthy urban families. We may see connections here with the emergence of anorexia in the 1980s in terms of social location but it is unwise to make too much of it at this stage. Walker Bynum suggests that there is evidence that these women clashed with their families over matters related to marriage, in other words about their position in society, and particularly their autonomy.[23] While these women may have been using the control of food to establish their place in society beyond the boundaries of marriage, they also used the symbolism of food to talk of their desire for God. This imagery was largely taken from the Song of Songs with its very sexual and sensual use of food to express the love and desire between two very earthly lovers. In other words they were expressing the opinion that God was known through the senses and so many mystics spoke of tasting God, of feeding on God and of devouring the divine. Hadewijch understood the food given in the Eucharist to be both erotic and nurturing and an event in which she would eat and be eaten. This symbolised the interpenetration and mutual engulfing that she saw as necessary in order to truly love the God who was made man.[24] For her and for many other women of the period to love meant that one's body became food for another and she spoke of her desire being a hunger of the soul for God.

Walker Bynum sees it as quite natural that women would focus on food in the religious realm since it was also very important and quite defining for them in the social arena. There was a public acknowledgement of this by men who exhibited fear of the power that women could exert through their control of food and, as may be expected, there was much talk of magic being carried out in food preparation. This was power indeed, and so an ideal arena in which women could make meaningful gestures. Walker Bynum suggests that these gestures influenced families, church hierarchies and perhaps even God. Women found themselves in a strange position: they did have influence over food within their households, but they also received cultural messages about feeding others and not themselves, and these were overlaid with religious messages also. As early as the time of Jerome women had been warned about the lustful properties of food so that even married women were warned to take care. Mary of Oignies was so afraid of sensation that she prayed that God would take away her sense of taste.[25] In addition it had been noted by spiritual directors that control of food also made menstruation stop, and while there was not as much disease with it as in earlier times there was not exactly comfort, so its ceasing was seen as a good thing, one form of pollution being overcome through the exercise of another form of discipline. As an aside it is also worth noting that women who fasted were said to have sweet breath and to no longer excrete – both these aspects made them objects of admiration.

Walker Bynum reminds us that we must take into account the more general medieval spiritual world when considering the way in which women used food as part of their discipline. This was a world that understood physical punishment as an imitation of

Christ and therefore as a worthy pursuit and not as a self-punishment at all. Of course it also carried with it great gain and some of that could be seen in the here and now: the bodies of holy women were said to lactate or to exude miraculous fluids. So a profound transformation came over them – they no longer exuded those things considered defiling, menstrual blood and excrement, but rather sweet odors and breast milk, the latter being believed to have healing properties. It is interesting to note that male mystics often had images of being suckled, while the women often saw themselves as the ones who gave suck. This is profoundly important when we also realize that Christ himself was understood to lactate and to feed his followers in this way.[26] It could be argued then that the women, in seeing themselves as a source of food in this way, were also imitating Christ, perhaps more than imitating, possibly even identifying with Christ. Not only does it offer a picture of Christ represented as mother, an image that had been in theological currency for some time – Clement of Alexandria had spoken of Christ in this way as early as the second century[27] – but it also enabled the metaphor to work the other way and allowed women to claim Christic significance. This is a strong statement of identity in a world that preferred passive and defined women.

Walker Bynum also points out that the lactating Virgin was also associated with the Eucharist in medieval art as food for the soul.[28] So then by association the lactating breasts of holy women were also understood to be healing food for the soul and the body, there are many tales of people going on pilgrimage to suck at the breasts of holy women. There is an interesting reversal apparent with these women: they gave up or severely restricted their food intake in order that they might become food for others. Perhaps many modern day mothers would understand this reversal as they feed their children first from their own bodies and then from their tables while holding back themselves, because of either scarcity of resources or a fear of what ingesting that food might do to them – less demonic possession than inches on the hips. Walker Bynum reminds us that the wound in the side of Christ was often imaged as a breast;[29] it was also often depicted as a semi-open vulva, which is perhaps not so significant in this argument. When considering art of the period Bynum gives some interesting interpretations to many of the pictures that scholars such as Steinberg see in purely phallocentric terms. For example, *Christ with ear of wheat and grape vine* (Friedrich Herlin School, 1469) is viewed as portraying Christ as food and thus equating him with a woman. She illustrates that Christ is understood to lactate, to offer his breast as food and to possess a womb into which believers may enter for rest. This kind of iconography lends weight to the argument that many of the women of this period who were reported to lactate like Christ could be understood to be offering their breast milk to the faithful as an embodied sacrament. In that way they became the Christ for those who received this soothing sacrament, they embodied Christ in the here and now. Although it was most usually women who offered their breasts in this way, Bernard of Clairvaux offered his breast to his novices as a suckling mother; at his breast they gain comfort and the love of God. Bernard was rather an exception to the rule.

Bynum believes that the theology of the period wished to emphasise the role of Jesus as mediator in joining our substance to divinity[30] through this two-way ingestion process. At this time Mary was understood as the flesh of Christ and so her mothering role was also incorporated into the holy women's understanding of spirituality. Bynum is suggesting that the representations of the body of Christ can be seen as moments of symbolic reversal in which role and status are overturned and normal structures thrown to the wind. She says this is nowhere clearer than in the Eucharist, where what women are supposed to be is publicly inverted. Christ on the cross and offered in the Mass did not and does not become a King but rather a lactating and birthing mother, while the male priest becomes the food-preparer, a role quite unlike that of a male in society.[31] Of course, this reversal is not necessarily a good thing since it can also be the incorporation of the female role by a male in order to remove real women altogether from the sacramental frame.[32] After all, despite the portrayal of Christ as the lactating mother, and women's own ability to lactate for the faithful as well, women still spoke of themselves in relation to a male God.

Bell suggests that the holy anorexics of the later Middle Ages make it plain that the business of being female deserves attention, and he concludes that gender struggles underlie the relationship between women and food in whatever century we observe it. Walker Bynum would agree that women, through their control of food, controlled much more besides, for example their families and even clerical authorities, since they were able to claim visions that challenged the central control of the church. She notes that in rejecting the family meal a person is also able to critique the whole notion of family and it does seem that many of the women who restricted their food intake were in just such a critical position. Were they then rejecting one central pillar of a patriarchal society, as many modern scholars suggest the anorexics of today do? Walker Bynum is not so sure, as she sees the relevance and symbolic capital of food for medieval women as being much richer than it is for women today. She argues that the food behaviour of these women was about service to others as well as self-discipline. They did after all feed the poor while not eating themselves, their rituals did involve eating as well as abstaining. As Walker Bynum puts it, 'Through fasting women internalized as well as manipulated and escaped patriarchal familial and religious structures. But the self starvation of some thirteenth, fourteenth and fifteenth century women had a resonance and a complexity that are not captured by the analogy to modern disease entities.'[33] She accuses the modern world of having narrow and one-dimensional understandings of food and the body. While she acknowledges, as the quote shows, the oppression of women through clerical and cultural attitudes she also shows how women understood food to be a source of life and positive sensation. Walker Bynum suggests that we think again about the way we understand food and perhaps actually gain something from the medieval understanding. We appear to fear food and so want to fix eating disorders by looking at issues of control rather than at the glorious fact of embodiment and the place of food within that as a sensuous joy. While we continue to understand food only in terms of control then we also understand that we can never have the kind of control that we wish and this in turn, she argues, makes us violent towards those things we fear because we can not control them. To the forefront in this war are the bodies of women, which seem to be the most unpredictable and least controllable. A complex picture, then, is emerging when we consider the relationship of women and food and we have not yet looked at how the Protestant world has viewed these matters.

Food and the Reformers

We should not be surprised to see that there are few links between the way in which the medieval women understood fasting and the way that the later Protestant Reformers understood it. They would have had a great reluctance to be associated with anything Catholic and indeed guarded their distinct identity very closely, which may prove interesting when we consider the now familiar issue of bodies and boundaries. They also did not have the same eucharistic framework in which to understand the matter of food and so it would seem likely that they developed along quite different lines. However, once again we see that the body and what goes into it becomes a symbolic matter way beyond what is actually contained in the substances and the actions themselves. The body once more becomes a foundational matter and exclusions and inclusions are decided concerning its appearance and size. The sixteenth and seventeenth centuries saw the understanding of the human body and the self within it shift to that of ordered systems that were made up of mechanical parts governed by laws and reason. The body was then passive and needed rational mastery and control.

In addition to rejecting the practices that came before them the Protestant Reformers also found it necessary to have some biblical grounds for fasting, and they found very few in the Christian scriptures, Matthew 9:14–15 being about the most obvious. Having found a text, they also had to deal with the question of when and how they should do this. Their view of the place of the body in salvation was different from that of their Catholic forebears – they had after all actively encouraged marriage and the creation of families rather than celibacy and the solitary or monastic life. Luther was never that happy with the idea of sex but he did say that within marriage God would wink at it. So when they did turn to the matter of food they had to decide whether mortification of the flesh was necessary in this way and if so what it might mean for them. What was certain was that a theological rethink was required. The first step was to see a distinction between fasting that was generally good for a person, and religious fasting that was still connected to religious festivals or times of penitence, be they public or private. All the time there was great care not to be too close to Catholic ideas on these matters.

There was some variation in the way the different Protestant groups used and understood fasting, but it is not my intention to deal with this in any great detail here; a few examples will do. The Puritans did not understand fasting to aid salvation in any way but they did use it as a political tool by congregations, either for some general political aim or to make sinners within the fold repent. This may seem like a rather aggressive form of fasting, psychological blackmail particularly towards individuals who could see their friends going hungry, but they did also believe that it made prayer more fervent and that God would more easily answer these prayers offered on empty stomachs. Ministers and doctors also prescribed fasting for melancholy and madness, which is rather strange, given the effects of lack of food, and attests to their belief that fasting was curative. It has been suggested that this approach for these ailments may have developed because Catholic exorcism was no longer available.[34] I think this is a point to remember when we look later at the modern diet industry, even that beyond the religious diet industry. What they all appear to offer is some form of healing from a desperately disordered and unhappy life to a more meaningful, fulfilled and righteous one through the overcoming of one's demons. In this way, then, there is still the suggestion that dieting is curative and salvific, even if the prayer aspect has been dropped.

While the idea of salvation through fasting was not to the forefront with Protestants there does seem to be a discernible train of thought in the area of fasting and spiritual purity, but there were diverse views. The early Methodists kept a weekly fast which was meant to be an act of will that actually would in time erase the will. They also emphasised the health benefits of a weekly fast. Some Presbyterian thinkers also agreed that fasting was a benefit to the health but it soon fell out of favour with them as many of the leading thinkers felt that it was too like Catholicism and Methodism to be correct.[35] Along with the notion that it was 'pagan' there was a mounting suspicion amongst many

Protestant groups that it actually depleted strength and so was to be avoided. Many Methodists did continue to see fasting as a positive practice and they even argued that if people were too heavy then they could not hear sermons properly and of course could not be spiritually uplifted. The notion that less weight equalled more spirit was set well and truly in place by these groups, thus placing the regulation of size in the framework of religious observance. For some thinkers this was taken further and fat was associated with evil and horror, sin and corruption.[36] Those who have seen the film *Babette's Feast* will have some understanding of the concern and suspicion with which food was viewed. In the film, the small Protestant group who live on ill-cooked food have to agree that they would not enjoy the great feast cooked for them by the 'foreigner', Babette, who placed before them food that they had never seen before. Babette, as the hostess, gains great satisfaction from entertaining so lavishly, indeed in the end bankrupting herself through her generosity, her self-giving. She pours herself out in the care and passion with which she prepares the feast for what she knows will be a rather undiscerning and perhaps resistant group. The Christic dimensions of this character cannot be overlooked and the utopian Messianic Banquet is always before the viewers' eyes. In the film as in the gospels it is a banquet that has reluctant and half-knowing guests; those who when offered life in abundance through the sensual delights of food and company are not quite sure what to do with it and are even suspicious of it. What is so telling in the film is the way in which their pious intentions yet mean spirits become transformed as they enter into the 'sin' of enjoying the food and leave the table happy and less mean-spirited.

Beware of the flesh!

Along with R. Marie Griffith I wish to focus the rest of my attention in this chapter on how Protestant thought on food and fasting developed mainly in the United States in order to set the scene for the main part of the investigation in the next chapter. Griffith shows that groups such as the Mormons appeared to have a much more level approach to fasting by suggesting that people restrict their intake in order to offer to the poor whatever money they would have spent on food. This notion of fasting and social activism is not an unfamiliar one to us today, particularly during Lent. In the mid eighteenth century Benjamin Rush raised the connection between eating and ecology;[37] he suggested that nature was put under strain by constantly having to fulfil the demand for food that humans make, and therefore regulating food intake took on a much broader significance than it had to date. It has to be said that this idea did not find widespread acceptance, but at least it had entered the discourse.

Always lurking in the discourse was the idea that the body is a great deceiver, a delusion which actually perverts the will of God. In short, then, in matters of food as of sex the body is not to be trusted and has to be 'done unto' rather than allowed to speak its own needs and desires. To this general view in the mid nineteenth century Elizabeth Towne[38] added a rather startling idea. She believed that food was to do with incarnating ideas, that like all forms of matter it held ideas. It followed, therefore, that one's own body would be affected by the dead matter and half-dead thoughts that one ingested. We could literally become clogged up by other thoughts that would be transmitted to us by the dead matter we ate. This is perhaps taking the notion of 'we are what we eat' to extremes but, again, there is perhaps a noticeable trajectory from the Catholic saints who would eat nothing but the host to this kind of thinking. They did not believe that they ingested dead ideas and matter but rather that the Body of Christ was the only necessary food being, as it was, pure and full of light. For Towne it was important that we should not be dull and dense with dead thoughts so that we could function better in the world. In this way she is in line with other thinkers of the late nineteenth and early twentieth centuries who believed that regulating food intake would not only make us vital individuals but crucially that this would in turn make us financially and socially successful.[39] Here is a turn that the Catholic saints before could not have anticipated. Certainly one could argue that many of them fasted in order to be thought well of in society, but it is hard to argue that they financially benefited from this way of life.

Once it was suggested that how one ate affected one's chances in life, women bore a heavy responsibility to see that their children learned the correct eating habits and thus gained advantage in life. More than this, at its most extreme there was also a racial element to the argument as women became responsible for making sure that the race itself was invigorated through providing the right kind and amount of food for their white children who had racial as well as social duties to perform.[40] As the body becomes seen as social and financial destiny rather than spiritual destiny, which was always dualistic in nature and placed women on the back foot, we might expect to find a less gendered approach developing, but we would be wrong. Fasting and self-control in eating matters was not just a way to cleanse oneself but also to 'overcome all that was debilitating and feminizing about modern civilization'.[41] So again we see that hidden in the rhetoric is the idea that the female body with its natural softness and curves is somehow debilitated and 'soft' in ways beyond its texture. I find myself agreeing with William James who noticed that the effect of theological suppositions on the stomachs of believers was extraordinary,[42] and I wish to add that these presuppositions had dramatic effects in the lives of women whose natural bodies would never actually mirror the kind of heaven that these male thinkers devised. In addition they, like Eve, would also be responsible and, by extension, guilty, in relation to the eating habits of others.

Within the United States' context there is a noticeable exception to this restricted eating code and interestingly it comes from a black Pentecostal church. In the 1930s Father Divine[43] preached a gospel of food as a concrete example of heavenly love. His church understood Holy Communion as a banquet and the church also dedicated itself to feeding people, not just the needy – all the followers were fed free. The purpose of having a living body and soul was to receive the love of God through the beauty of God's bounty. Any restriction or rejection of this was understood as a rejection of God. Keeping body and soul together was not a mere phrase for Father Divine, but the basis of his understanding of the gospel message of incarnation. He was a rotund man who was exceptionally healthy and he proclaimed that abundant food was a miracle and should be embraced. His theology was not simply based on that of taking care of the hungry, that is to say, he felt food was there to be indulged in by all and so his mission was to feed the five thousand. There is something very challenging in his theology, which acknowledges God in all matter so that the ingestion of food, far from being evil, sinful and corrupt, was seen as the ingestion of not only God's bounty but in some way God himself. I am sure he would not have said so, but here appears to be a truly incarnational view of religion in which the God of abundant life is in each mouthful of food, the ecological God is ingested with each grain and the believer is called to indulge.

All theology is contextual, or so I believe, and so it is interesting to understand that Father Divine's mother was a slave. Like many freed slaves she gained weight and indeed it has been argued that Father Divine developed the view he did because of his mother's history. It is more than likely that he did, but what is it we are saying in this? Access to food has always been in the hands of the wealthy and so in many ways it is only the privileged that can worry about it. For most people throughout history the problem has been lack of food. When it was available the vast majority made the most of it because it was hard to tell when it would be available again. This is no less true for those who were slaves. Yes, they needed to be kept alive, but they should also not cost too much to keep. Ignoring for the moment that there may be more to freed slaves gaining weight than access to food, we can begin to see the politics behind the theology that Father Divine created. If weight could be a sign of the survival, indeed victory, of people over poverty and slavery, then it also became a very powerful theological metaphor. In addition, fat bodies did not speak of obedient bodies but rather bodies that literally pleased themselves, comforted and indulged themselves, not a reality that most slaves would have known. Pleasure and food were blessings bestowed by a loving God and his grateful children should not reject his bounty. Perhaps another point that could be made is that the generation of freed slaves in the United States understood themselves to be redeemed in their lives, thus placing less emphasis on the need to prepare their souls through regulation. They had lived much regulated lives and prayed to be free so they could wear the freedom on their bodies just as their slavery had been imposed on their bodies.[44] This will be a theme that I will develop when considering the way in which we might think of a Fat Jesus in relation to global capitalism.

I think a number of things have come to light in this chapter which help the consideration of women and food and the possible creation of a Fat Jesus. It is obvious that we have a biblical picture that certainly does speak about fasting but in the main speaks about food and the sensory pleasures of it as well as the divine blessing bestowed through it. The question then arises where the Christian tradition found its restricting attitude to food, and I think that this has also come to light as a legacy of the Church Fathers. We have also seen how food is indeed a gendered phenomenon in Christian discourses and the ways in which women and men engaged with it are quite distinct. Just as with celibacy,[45] where women and men while sharing the same tradition came to different understandings, so with food and fasting. Further, how men understood this for women and how women understood it for themselves are not always the same. I am not claiming any hard and fast rules here, but rather suggesting that there may be resources in our Christian past that both help women understand their present-day relationship with food, and also help to develop another understanding of the bodies of women as enfleshed resisters of patriarchal narratives. This latter scenario is of much importance for an incarnational religion.

I find it very illuminating to consider the ways in which Catholicism with its high eucharistic tradition is able to offer women a way of understanding themselves as Christ in their bodies, a possibility denied their Protestant sisters. In terms of developing a Fat Jesus, the Eucharist and the cross-over between women and the body of Christ makes an interesting pondering point. How Father Divine, another marginalised person, was able to understand his body as that of Christ is also very compelling. The emerging discourse of the controlled and regulated body and social and financial advantage is of extreme importance in developing a fat Christology. For the moment all these points need to be noted as possible building blocks in the chapters to come. In the next chapter I want to take a more in-depth look at the way in which the twentieth century has seen an explosion of Christian dieting and to consider the theological justification behind such an explosion. Are we simply witnessing secular culture affecting Christians and Christians in turn attempting to find theological justification or is it the reverse, that what we see in the secular world is simply the inevitable result of our Christian heritage with its body-regulating obsession?

Chapter Three

'Slim For Him' [1]

It is in part the anxiety of being a woman that devastates the feminine body.[2]

I do not wish to make this chapter a comparison between Christian and Jewish approaches to food but I can not resist the recent paraphrase I heard regarding Jewish ideas of food. It goes like this: they hate us, they tried to kill us, they failed, let's eat! In the light of the complex picture emerging in the last chapter this appears refreshingly simple and indeed very biblical – if you are going to bake cakes for the Queen of Heaven then why not eat them just to celebrate being alive? In this chapter I want to look more closely at some ways in which the late nineteenth century and the twentieth century were affected by the dieting culture, particularly the religious dieting culture. For some of the nineteenth century slimness was seen as unhealthy, but we also see the emergence of another rhetoric under the weight of evangelical religion which demonised obesity. This was allied to a public/ private split, with women in the theatre being praised for being voluptuous, while of course their virtue was often called into question, and women at home being praised for being frail and ethereal. This helps us understand that women's bodies,under the male gaze, have very different purposes and are expected to fit the different requirements. This was also a time when living skeletons were very popular in freak shows; these people were usually men and often found to be infected with tapeworm. Although this was a form of what may be called commercial fasting, as we shall see, this was not unknown within a religious context also.

Communal fasting

When it took a religious turn, the fasters were normally girls and women; for example, the Dutch girl Engeltje van der Vlies was visited by one thousand people and was listed in the English travellers' guide, a book that signposted places of interest for the English tourist abroad. Closer to home there was Ann Moore of Tutbury who was an impoverished mother of two when she stopped eating in 1807. She claimed she had been overcome with revulsion for food when changing the sheets of the bed of her employer, who was also the father of her children. As she refrained from food she became very religious and indeed began to gain a reputation as a mystic, which proved to be a rather lucrative way of life – certainly better than being a housemaid and concubine.[3] She became famous but in this new age where science was emerging and men did not like a challenge to their learning and their moral pronouncements, she was put under watch for fraud and indeed was found to be eating. There were many such 'miraculous maidens' who survived on water or perhaps a little bread also, and they were seen as a curiosity as much as a religious phenomenon. One such was the so-called Welsh fasting girl, Sarah Jacob, who is reported to have awoken one February morning in 1867 with a sharp pain in her stomach and by the time she returned from school she was doubled up in agony. She never returned to school and her fame began. Although she was attended by a doctor who would have been aware of the psychological as well as physical reasons being put forward for a range of illnesses in young girls, Sarah was never diagnosed with any illness. Her fits and paralysis would normally have pointed the medic of the day to look at the whole question of her dawning adolescence and the question of whether masturbation was the cause of the problems and clitoridectomy the cure.[4] Perhaps masturbation in these young women was less the problem than their dawning awareness that as they approached adulthood their options were very limited and perhaps piety offered the wider choice.

Sarah Jacob gained a great deal of attention through her (at first) limited food intake. She stopped eating altogether in October 1867, and people came from as far as London to be in the presence of this little girl. Of course there was a cultural aspect to this sideshow mentality. Wales was in those days part of what the English saw as a disappearing world and the quaintness of the environment and the language made the trip even more exotic. The arrivals at the newly opened Pencader station would be taken by cart to the farmhouse. The whole experience would be of entering a world unlike the one they had known. This was a world in which grown men still believed they could step into a fairy ring and disappear, and some thought that Sarah had done just that, and this was the reason for her inability to eat. Sarah herself increasingly understood her inability to eat within a Christian convention of piety and those who visited her were often treated to her reading from the Bible or reciting her own religious poetry. The Jacob family were Nonconformist, but Sarah it seems was received into the Anglican Church at her request. Her family's acceptance of this may have had more to do with their own social aspirations than any religious tolerance; it was accepted that any Welsh person who wished to develop a career or move upwards socially had to become Anglican, and the Jacob family were certainly on the up before their daughter became a curio but most definitely afterwards. Pragmatism it may have been, or perhaps opportunism. It has to be said the Anglican minister was more than delighted to receive such a celebrity into his congregation.

The visitors who flocked to see this curious child came from a much more modern world and really must have felt propelled back in time. They did, however, show their appreciation for this experience through financial gifts. The whole area benefited from the attention with business thriving from the influx of visitors. But there is no happy outcome to this story. Some suspicion did arise and the child was watched for several days by a team of nurses, as a result of which she died. The unfortunate parents, but not the medics or clerics involved, were had up for manslaughter and sent to prison. Sarah was given many opportunities to eat and drink and she refused them all. It was commonly held, by those who refused to believe she was totally deceitful, that she was suffering from hysteria, while some believed that it was her being watched that caused intolerable stress leading to her death.

How we begin to understand this behaviour, and that of the

many other women and girls who choose the same path, is still a matter of debate. It has to be acknowledged that women at the end of the nineteenth century were faced with very conflicting images which it can be argued led to the manifestation of strange phenomena. Women of this time regularly got 'the vapours' within a family setting that was both intimate and controlling, a setting in which 'unconditional loyalty does not allow personal autonomy, romantic love does not tolerate open conflict and moral self discipline represses every frustration'.[5] It can be argued that the family meal would under these conditions become a battleground due to its metaphoric significance as the centre of family life. At this table women acted out their restricted roles and children learnt that food refusal was rebellion. As always there has to be a class dimension to this; nevertheless we see that there were issues around food for women of this period that were not purely religious in the way they may have been understood to be for medieval women. It was more likely to be the strong daughters of the urban elite who, subjected to the new medicalisation of restricting women's food intake, found them- selves diagnosed with 'the new disease'. Joan Jacobs Brumberg argues that the shift from saint to patient was indeed shaped by a specific intersection of class and gender which took place around the 1870s. While the urban elite were being diagnosed, their rural less educated sisters were still having 'religious experiences' in which they spoke of other-worldly power juxtaposed with little or no power in this world.[6] Perhaps the case of Sarah Jacob illus- trates the way in which this was slowly changing. While she lived there was no attempt to create a medical explanation, yet when she died her family were prosecuted and subsequent explana- tions were very much medical in nature. It is true to say that Victorian femininity was itself judged by what one consumed and this too was highly influenced by class. A women's desire to eat was seen as a way of judging her sexual desire also – hence voluptuous actresses and slender wives – and the ability not to eat was seen as a middle-class accomplishment through which one distinguished oneself from the lower classes. So as ever there are many layers of meaning and significance tied up in the matter of what women eat.

From Christic icon to media image

It is generally supposed that the religious significance of food restriction died away at the turn of the twentieth century to be replaced by the purely medical model, but this is not entirely the case. That is to say, the rhetoric of the mystery value of food and its qualities beyond the purely calorific did persist – as indeed it still does today, it could be argued. At approximately the same time as Sarah Jacob was starving to death William Banting[7] was amongst the first to talk of reducing and suggesting that food had hidden virtues: that there were good calories and bad calories. Interestingly Banting at first aimed his new ideas at the poor immigrants into North America, particularly the Irish and Italians, but with the development and growth of food corporations his classification of good food and bad food caught on as creative marketing techniques. Food now could lend itself to a social purity rhetoric in the same way as it had always lent itself to a religious one. In this way, then, it could be argued that the religious underpinning of the food rhetoric was never truly left behind. Returning to Mary Douglas once more, it can be argued that 'one of the most obvious forms of religious behaviour ... is the use of bodily symbols to express the notion of an organic social system'.[8] What we see happening is a social rhetoric that prides itself on being medical and therefore objective, but is very closely allied to the worst restrictions of the Christian heritage. (I always wonder how might it have been for women's bodies if the Goddess had been our heritage?) Recognising this is significant for two reasons: first, it enables us to understand the origins and, second, once we see the roots we can feel the tree. Well, perhaps we can stake it to grow in a more advantageous way! Women's magazines may have taken the place of spiritual directors and lectionaries but the model of the ideal woman is just as fixed as it was for our foresisters. This is neither a conscious nor an unconscious process – it is, most worryingly, habitual. It bypasses thought in a way that was not that of our foresisters. Theirs was a religious discipline and so required of them mental commitment, thought and reflection in a way that women's magazines do not encourage or indeed require. Certainly it is true to say that images of the ideal woman are not altogether fixed, yet they are also not open to interpretation because they have moved beyond the interpretative to become the 'given', and this given nature is centuries old, based in the 'law' that women's bodies will be moulded by outside forces and women will comply. This compliance, like many forms of abuse, is almost welcomed since it gives women an image through which they can mediate their meaning in the world, through which they can contain uncertainty, longing and pain. With the demise of religion we still witness the 'religious longing' – the search for meaning – and the bodies of women are still the significant conveyers of that meaning for society. (I will address the question of the bodies of women and the way in which they bear the weight of male and, by extension, cultural expectation later.)

Christian women have always relied on visual images in their search for identity and we have no reason to suppose this way of searching is not as important today. What has happened, though, which incarnational theologians need to be concerned about, is that the identity has, through the normalising techniques of modern science, been reduced to the edges of the skin.[9] Bodies come to be seen as mirrors to the self and no more. They lose in that way their truly incarnational potential and become indicators of individual moral virtue, conveyers of already worked out social control. They become objects rather than the glorious outpouring of the divine/human dance, which is best danced in the veil of constantly reflective and increasingly desiring subjectivity. The new salvation is very narrow in ideal and practice and so 'helps sustain a sociosymbolic system that fails to nourish the diversity and complexity of human search for meaning'.[10] Women are trapped in the habitual images rather than being the radiant icons of divine power which they are born to be when they live from passion and desire. Incarnational theology would therefore call for a disruption of the visual conventions and narratives that are placed before women and instead allow women to feel their own divine becoming through their skins. This is no narrow call for individual flourishing: it is a political challenge to tight economic and social control in its diverse and global manifestations. As we shall see, this does not appear to be the call that most Christian dieting regimes are making.

Despite the secular forgetting of the Christian narrative at the heart of their views of size, there was always a strand of religious thought that dealt with food and size. As we have noted, Banting introduced the idea that food had good and bad qualities and this was carried into the twentieth century. It became interlinked with the discourse on 'lean and mean' which developed in the 1920s when fat was understood as dead weight and seen as a hindrance to thought and progress. This slim and efficient model was to remain in vogue for much of the twentieth century although, as we have seen, the wars did create a need to have curvy women who could be understood culturally as the nurturers of a nation in need. Alongside the desire for slim and efficient figures there was also a rhetoric of punishment for those who did not fit the bill. They would be ugly, ill and die young – no judgement there then!

Give me that 'Weigh Down' religion!

It was not really until the 1950s that the explicit link between size and religion once again raised its head and this time it was well and truly a Protestant phenomenon with all the trademarks that one would expect. In 1957, Charlie Shedd[11] wrote a book entitled *Pray Your Weight Away*, in which it is claimed that fatties are people who literally can weigh their sin. Fat, he argued, is the embodiment of disobedience to God since it prohibits the Holy Spirit from penetrating one's heart – it can not get through the layers of fat. Shedd says that God did not ever imagine fat and his justification for this statement is that the slender are those who succeed in the world. At this early stage the huge responsibility of women in this matter was emerging because Shedd dedicates six chapters of his book to explaining how women ruin other people's diets through their out-of-control gluttonous behaviour. Mothers are particularly to blame in his view since they set in place very sinful patterns in their children; they are the ruin of their children. Victor Kane, some ten years later in his *Devotion for Dieters*, was declaring that our birthright is to be firm, hard and godly, not flabby. Here we see again the phallic God of whom Nelson speaks, writ large on the bodies and in the psyches of believers. What is quite striking is that amidst the rhetoric of food being of the devil, there is no mention of the starving. It does not seem inconceivable to have a balancing rhetoric about sharing if one is to suggest that eating too much is a sin. However, there is absolutely no mention of this wider point – the purpose of restraint in eating is to overcome the devil in a very personal way, with no social analysis at all.

Among the books that appeared at this time were the strangely named *Jesus Diet for your Sins* and *Heal Yourself for Christ's Sake*, both of which claimed that the dieter would be more use to God the slimmer they became, because the path is narrow and one has to be thin to be able to get along it. As amusing as this may seem, there was no humour intended. Two books that appeared in the 1970s, Joan Cavanagh's *More of Jesus; Less of Me* and C. S. Lovett's *Help Lord, the Devil Wants Me Fat*, both sold 100,000 copies[12] each, signalling in a rather worrying way that this strange theology had a following. Lovett tells us that diets do not work because they come at the problem from the outside when actually it is the devil holding us internally captive. A short fast rectifies this by breaking the hold of the devil and then a diet will work because the Holy Spirit is now inhabiting the place where the devil once was. This is a perverse theology of 'food demons' that it is hard to believe people accept in the twentieth and twenty-first centuries, but they do. This can be further attested by the fact that by 1981 there were five thousand churches and 100,000 participants in the new 3D ('Diet, Discipline, Discipleship') programme that replaced Weight Watchers for the religious. This was a programme set up by Carol Showalter in 1973 and was one of a number of such programmes aimed at overcoming the sin of fatness. So seriously was fat seen as sin, that the Overeaters Victorious programme set up in Minnesota in 1977 had to close in shame when the founder Neva Coyle gained weight.[13] These groups could not be led by sinners. Other groups such as 'Step Forward and Jesus is the Weigh' give a hint through their names of their theological underpinning. All one has to do is step up to Jesus and he becomes all in all for a person who no longer needs to eat excessively, the converse of this being that if one fails to lose weight then faith, not metabolism, is the issue. They do not exactly resort to knocking out people's front teeth as in days of old but the guilt and shame are perhaps more crippling. One of the most successful groups has been 'First Place', which has a simple theology: put God first and the weight will drop off.

In addition to the diet regimes there are also the religious fitness regimes with names such as 'Praise Aerobics' and 'Fit for God', the latter telling would-be participants that in this eight-week plan you will kick the devil out and invite health and fitness in. The language is telling: God here is replaced by health and fitness with such ease that the reader is left in little doubt that the two are actually the same. In his book *What Would Jesus Eat? The Ultimate Programme for Eating Well, Feeling Great and Living Longer*[14] (the last being an odd desire for those keen to meet their saviour), Don Colbert tells us that fat is not a good Christian witness since food is an instrument of the devil. He is an expert on holy eating, or so it seems, as he takes us through what Jesus would have eaten. You won't find salt and pepper on his table, we are told, and lobster – he would not touch it. However, he will reveal Jesus' favourite food of all time in Chapter 2 of his book as well as discussing the health compounds found in the fish from Galilee. There is a whole chapter dedicated to healthy biblical snacks and a guide to eating out the Jesus way. His main contention is that Jesus ate a healthy diet of vegetables, fish and occasional meat with a lot of water and some wine. (This is contested by biblical scholars, who claim that the average peasant at the time of Jesus would have lived on bread with some bits of fish as a garnish but this does not stand in the way of Don Colbert.) He like many others is more concerned with the power of the devil in food matters and less concerned with accurate historical depictions and he wants to see the fat punished for being so open to the devil. Needless to say, God does not let him down, ensuring that those who indulge in greed and gluttony do not live long, they live in bondage and they die young in guilt. The saved are doing their best to help the weak through the creation of such helpful things as fitness videos, which make clear their intention with names like 'Fit for Christ', and which can all be purchased from faithfullyfit.com. Naturally there were varying degrees of theological strangeness in this movement and Hal Lindsey with his *Late Great Planet Earth* was amongst the strangest. His theology was what may be called extreme realised eschatology: if you do not like your body in the here and now, no need to wait until after death to get a new one: you can have one now through the power of prayer and the gift of salvation, and then eat all you want and not gain weight.[15] With the exception of this movement, most of those set up in the 1970s and before were very strong on the language of punishment and condemnation for being fat.

With the move into the 1980s much of the language changed, although I wish to argue that the fundamental message remained the same. It was in 1986 that the Weigh Down Workshops[16] were set up in Nashville by Gwen Shamblin and this has been the most successful Christian diet industry to date. Interestingly, this was a secular programme in origin and became Christian in the 1980s when it developed a Bible study course over twelve weeks which was designed to fill your spiritual hunger and make you thin. The founder tells us that she went from a dumpy 125 pounds to 107 pounds through the power of the Bible study. Too much food is clearly disobedience to God, and this particular disobedience was, in Shamblin's view, the reason for the devastation of 9/11.[17] The punishment model then appears to be alive and well in Shamblin's theology.

Despite this rather provocative approach it is fair to say that the language of most of the 1980s religious diet industry was more 'scientific' and medicalised. Indeed, the whole industry was becoming more professional and running along the lines of a corporate/therapeutic model. There is no conversion narrative in the stories told by the participants and the general approach in most of these programmes is simple – God wants you slim and so you have to do it. There is language rather like that used of sex and the similarities between some of these programmes and the 'True Love Waits'[18] programme are striking. We are told that eating can be an act of passion which carries many possibilities for regret and shame and the best way to ensure against this is to seek intimacy with God which will take the form of giving him total control. It is clear what kind of God is emerging here, the controller who does not like autonomy in his children, the one who punishes even with death those who have not got it right. This is not the kind of God that feminist liberation theology has been advocating for some decades now and it is hard to see how such a God could be viewed as a freer, which is indeed part of the rhetoric. We have the classic abuser who has the abused so fooled they believe the treatment is for their own good. Worse still from a feminist liberation point of view, what is emerging is the over-privatised God, the Me-me God, the one who cares about ME personally but does not seem to notice the starving.[19] A swing to this corporate yet totally individualistic God is a move in the right direction for those who wish to make money off the backs of others and a terrifying move for those who still believe in the world-transforming message of radical equality and mutuality that the gospels hold.

Just how far the religious underpinning of these diet groups is from a liberation theology can be seen by the language they use and the fanciful grasp of the Bible they appear to have. Mab Graff Hoover, one of the stalwarts of the religious diet industry, con-fides in us: 'When I look at chocolates or a beautiful birthday cake or Danish pastries it's hard for me to believe they are being offered through the Evil One. But I know from scripture that Satan continually tries to ruin the temple of God, the church, my body.' The diatribe goes on to reassure us that one can prevail through these comforting words: 'Today I will eat one piece of chicken, without the skin, a lot of salad, chewing it well, some vegetables, fruit and one small piece of bread. I will imitate the Lord.'[20] The certainty about Jesus' diet can be seen in other diet recipe books where we are told he was on a low-fat diet of locusts and honey along with lamb and yoghurt dressing. These insights are said to be biblical and are based on what is assumed to be the diet of Adam and Eve, the manna from heaven for the Israelites, Daniel eating vegetables and drinking water and John of course eating locusts and honey. They seem to have missed out all the feasting that also went on in the Bible, which I have mentioned in Chapter 2 as part of our heritage in these matters. Of course this insistence on knowing Jesus' diet serves the purpose of making these diets appear to be Christian, as opposed to simply secular diets that Christians follow. The reasons for this, one may argue, are not spiritual but rather financial – this is a multi-million-dollar industry. There is a huge market for Christian lifestyle products, books, magazines, jewellery, bumper stickers, videos, DVDs and diet groups. It is staggering to realise that 40 per cent of this huge market is given over to diet. Indeed in 2000 the esti-mated value of these Christian diet regimes was $77 billion and of course there will always be a market – as people generally gain more weight than they lose, there is a guaranteed clientele.

The naivety of these outpourings about the way in which Jesus ate and the demonic intentions behind birthday cake and chocolates would be pitiful except that they have many thousands in their grip and the flip side of imitating Jesus in his eating habits is the knowledge that one has in fact been overcome by the devil, and that death awaits. This is no simple-minded and harmless enterprise: it can itself seriously damage your health. This is a good time to mention that almost all these Christian diet groups are Protestant (there was one Catholic group in the USA but it folded almost as soon as opening, and almost all the people who attended were women). These women also give rather similar testimonies in the groups – they declare themselves to be weak foodaholics and often juxtapose this declaration with one about the strength of their husbands in this regard. Many are grateful that their menfolk actually reprimand them in food matters – this is seen as a blessing. The rhetoric is only too familiar to feminist liberation theologians, who have examined centuries of Christian history through which women have been kept in line by men through various means. When we are considering the issue of women and size we need to be mindful of the reasons that scholars have given (examined in Chapter 1) for the way women manifest in the world and then, perhaps, we will understand the harm that is being done to the bodies of women through the declarations of these virtuous men.

The website www.laymanstraining.com/weight provides the would-be patriarch with biblical eating habits to impose upon his family. This website has had 100,000 hits since it was set up in 1997 so is not exactly an obscure site. You are asked if you have the willpower of a saint and are quickly told that you do, and assured that within twenty-one days you will have incorporated biblical eating habits into your life. There are a number of affirmations that are said to help, such as 'because I belong to Jesus my flesh with its passions and desires is crucified. I walk by the spirit and do not carry out the desires of the flesh' (Galatians 5:24, 16). Alternatively there is 'Body and appetite settle down in the name of Jesus, conform to the Word of God'. There are practical tips too such as drinking a gallon of water a day and remembering that it is possible to call into being those things which do not exist (Romans 4:17b), and so repeating 'I have a flat stomach' will help. The purpose of all this is to reach peak performance in order to obey God. Many Bible passages are explained within the remit of dieting, such as Proverbs 23:2–3, 'Put a knife to your throat if you are a man of great appetite', which we are told means that food is treachery as it is one of Satan's tools to deceive and weaken the body in order that it may not serve Jesus efficiently. Psalm 141:3–4, 'Set a guard, O Lord, over my mouth; keep watch over the door of my lips ... do not let me eat their dainties', we are told is a warning against Satan's trap of junk food which raises sugar levels and depletes energy and leads to illness. Self-control, we are told, is our kingdom heritage and we should not give in to sugar. The website is full of such advice, including how to get a good night's sleep (Ecclesiastes 5:12): 'The full stomach of the rich man does not allow him to sleep.' This is accompanied by some suggestions for light snacks before bed and a warning that we will not function as we should if we do not have a good night's sleep. When so many are starving around the world I find this kind of website rather difficult to understand.

There is an even more worrying aspect to this diet industry: the true Christian woman is not only becoming narrower but also she has to be more beautiful if she is to truly reflect the heroic grandeur of her God. Along with the cookbooks, the devotional books and the fitness videos there are also the beauty books. They tell us that God is beautiful, healthy and vital and so the women who follow him also have to be; they must spend time each day making themselves as beautiful as they can as an advertisement for their God. Indeed, if they can provoke envy in other women this is a good thing as it may bring them to Christ in the hope that they too can look this good in Christ.[21] To look good is godly. Cynthia Culp Allen and Charity Allen Winters have written a book for the beauty-conscious Christian called *The Beautiful Balance of Body and Soul*, in which they provide Bible passages with each beauty tip. Their justification for writing the book is that they believe you would not wrap a priceless gift in a dingy grocery bag so 'why represent Jesus to others without looking confident, put together and beautifully appealing inside and out?'[22] Neva Coyle and Marie Chapian have added to this aspect of the industry with their book *Free to Be Thin* (I assume this was before Neva gained weight and brought shame on herself and the project!), in which they castigate women for the eating problems of the entire family, seeing it as the fault of a lazy and selfish homemaker. However, they end their book quoting from the Song of Songs telling the readers that once they have overcome the wickedness of overeating their reward will be to hear Jesus who will be saying, 'Behold you are beautiful, my love, behold you are beautiful. I will hie me to the mountain of myrrh and frankincense. You are all fair, my love, there is no flaw in you.'[23] The eroticism of these statements is never fully acknowledged and certainly the passion of the text itself is almost expunged by the sweet and innocent approach to what the text is actually suggesting. These Jesus dieters could never face that much embodied passion – it is after all what they are fighting through control of their appetites. There is, however, a bold message that just as God and Jesus are beautiful, so the good believer who has managed to overcome the demon in food will also be beautiful and this beauty will be physical and the cause of great admiration from Jesus himself. There will be no flaw in the true believer, a worrying statement of theology.

The connection between Jesus and physical beauty, health and vitality has a sinister reverse side: the way in which many of these fundamentalist Protestant groups view the matter of physical disability. In short they see it as demonic, which we can deduce from the way in which they represent health and fitness in their diet industries. As Christians have viewed God as perfect in every way, they have, to their eternal shame, viewed disability as imperfect and at times demonic. Women with disabilities have carried an extra burden since they are viewed as doubly transgressive. Many of those burnt as witches had no greater deformity than a third nipple, the so-called 'devil's teat'. The conflation of sin and disability is a devastating error that Christianity would do well to repent, but many of the groups I have looked at do not seem anywhere near such a repentance. Indeed they are vehement in their advocacy of the ideal, perfect, fit and healthy God who demands the same from his followers. What are his followers to do if they do not have it within their capacity to become the model of fully healthy and functioning people? I think a short look at some aspects of disabled theology will help highlight what I see as the theologically most unhealthy aspects of the fundamentalist Protestant obsession with size, shape and fitness.

Salvation beyond the edges

Nancy Eiesland is one of the first theologians to attempt to develop a theology of disability, and once again this is ahead of the churches, which have not really begun to grasp the issues involved in disabled civil rights. There is still, to their shame, reluctance in some churches to ordain people with disabilities. This is of course a direct result of viewing God as perfect and therefore insisting that his representatives also mirror that perfection. Eiesland urges 'acting out' which she describes as a theological method that joins political action with resymbolisation. It is the enactment of holding bodies together in societies filled with overt discrimination. The political action involves equal rights and access campaigning as well as face-to-face encounters with those who operate from the level of unthinking stereotypes. In short, acting out is the revolutionary work of resistance to acquiescence. This inevitably means coming to terms with bodies and their sometimes disagreeable aspects, and is not all celebration, demanding at times a huge price in terms of realistic engagement. Eiesland talks about 'survive-able' bodies, which are those that refuse to be self-flagellating because they do not fit the standard norm, instead learning to live with the pain and pleasure of being who they are. She rightly points out that in a society which wants us to engage with the obsessive quest for perfect bodies this act of self-worth and self-love is an act of resistance and liberation.

Fundamental to this process is solidarity with others who are disabled and a refusal to play the game of the 'good' and the 'bad' disabled. This sense of solidarity extends globally and poses questions about disability as a result of malnutrition or torture. It is thought that there are about 600 million people who are disabled worldwide and malnutrition is the cause of at least 20 per cent of it. We do not hear this in the rhetoric about food that the programmes I have examined provide. Indeed there is a deathly silence about matters of global food distribution since the focus is on the savable individual soul – as Jesus loves these people personally, so the devil attacks them personally, and this personal agenda gets in the way of thinking about the food needs of others. Of course it is also true to say (and I shall look at this in more detail later) that many of the occupations for which the Jesus diets are making one fit are just the kind that promote global inequalities rather than acting to alleviate them. So once again there are very profound theological questions to be asked of the Jesus dieters that they seem unable or unwilling to ask themselves. A theology of disability calls for relief from the causes of the pain and this involves calling for able-bodied and disabled alike to withdraw from death-dealing business and politics.

It is the disabled Christ who sits at the centre of this theology, and who acts as the moral imperative for these things to be striven for. God became flesh and flesh as we know comes in all shapes, sizes and with a wide range of ability and disability. For Eiesland it is the resurrected Christ who is a theological starting point since, 'in the resurrected Jesus Christ, they saw not the suffering servant for whom the last word was tragedy and sin, but the disabled God who embodied both impaired hands and feet and pierced side and the imago Dei'.[24]

In revealing a physically impaired resurrected body, all kinds of taboos are broken: the body that is impaired is not untouchable or unlovable – it is 'a new model of wholeness and a symbol of solidarity'.

Eiesland highlights how the disabled Christ also goes some way to alleviating the feminist concern over the maleness of Christ. The disabled Christ is not a suffering servant or an imperial Lord but rather is weak and an outcast. In addition the emphasis in this model is on physicality and not maleness. This Christ is not a 'fixer' either but is rather a survivor, which may be an encouraging image for some women.

The disabled Christ highlights the necessity for mutuality and interdependence, the latter being a condition of many disabled people. We are offered a Christ who needs care and mutuality for survival. Our society perpetuates the myth that the truly capable person needs no one and moves beyond interdependence; the disabled model challenges this and draws us back to humanity. Above all else the disabled Christ is a symbol 'of rightly ordered interpersonal and structural relations'.

Elizabeth Stuart picks up on Eiesland's claim that 'Jesus Christ the disabled God disorders the social-symbolic orders of what it means to be incarnate'.[25] Stuart finds this a profoundly challenging view and one that in her opinion opens the Christian debate to new and exciting possibilities. Along with Graham Ward she agrees that Jesus' body witnesses to many displacements, that is, incarnation, circumcision, transfiguration and resurrection all profoundly destabilise our idea of what materiality really is. The church as the body of Christ shares in a very unstable body, a body that calls all knowledge about bodies into question. In addition, according to Stuart Christians live in a world that they believe is in the process of redemption and so they have to live in critical connection with social constructions. Therefore, Christians will have radical views about beauty and perfect embodiment which will not conform to the dictates of heteropatriarchy in all its crushing reality. Stuart reflects on the experience of some disabled people who have different ideas about body boundaries. Many who use wheelchairs claim there is an invisible boundary between them and the chair; the same is the case for those with artificial limbs. This body boundary fluidity is, according to Stuart, a good model for Christ: the one who knows no fixed rules of matter and dissolves boundaries. Christians have had at the heart of their symbolic world a broken, tortured and displaced body, yet they have been slow to engage with this reality, living as they have done in the ivory tower of dualistic metaphysics.

It is this fluid and endlessly challenging God that we miss out on through the insistence on perfect bodies, perfect sizes and very narrow body boundaries. In a very literal way what these 'Jesus dieters' are doing is reducing the redemptive possibilities of the radical message of the gospels that in my view can not be reduced to scripture beauty tips and biblical eating habits. Indeed I am offended by such suggestions; they fail in my view to even begin to grasp the purpose of the Christian faith which is world-changing through mutuality and vulnerability, not through tight control and distrust of the body in which divine/human potential lies. The Jesus dieters and beautifiers have failed to understand that what they are conforming to, yet claiming they are not, is yet another divisive worldly hierarchy of worthy and unworthy beings, and in so doing they are sacrificing the radical potential of the gospel they claim to know so well. The gendered nature of this compliance with worldly hierarchy is of great concern since it delivers the bodies of women over to strict control and self-distrust which cannot in my view allow the full becoming of their divine natures. Women who are encouraged to believe that the devil wants them to eat and is lurking in every chocolate are not women who will value themselves as autonomous and powerful incarnations. Whether they succeed in becoming a holy size six or whether they fail, the damage is done, they are divided within themselves and encouraged to distrust their desires and to despise their weakness. This is a familiar pattern throughout Christian history in relation to women and one that feminist theology has worked on many fronts to overcome, but it has not until now given serious attention to this growing religious diet industry, and this has been a mistake. In addition they are re-instating the 'firm hard and up God' that Nelson has done so much to dethrone, through their insistence that firm bodies serve God the best. In reducing the relationship with God to the food we eat they also overemphasise the idea of willpower and have no place for vulnerability which the disabled Jesus shows as strength in the Christian God. What emerges is a hard-edged blamer rather than a permeable co-redeemer, a control freak rather than a passionate risk-taker who engages with the uncer-tainties of incarnation in order to empower the glorious bursting forth of the divine/human reality. All this is lost in the control rhetoric of the Jesus dieters, who believe that their salvation hinges on whether they eat cake or not. They look for a certain world and, as we know, such a world requires that the rigid boundaries we create around our bodies also extend to our lives, our countries and our religions. In my view this is not the message of incarnation – that could never emerge from the kind of theology that could develop Slim For Him programmes.

Small diets, big dollars

No examination of this multimillion dollar industry would be complete without a serious look at Gwen Shamblin's Weigh

Down programme which has to be the most successful of its kind. Shamblin hit the headlines with her bold assertion that fat people do not go to heaven because 'grace does not go down to the pig-pen'.[26] In short, then, Shamblin was offering slim hips and eternal salvation because of her contention that the fatness of Americans is due to a profound spiritual crisis. Her book *The Weigh Down Diet* has sold millions of copies and the twelve-week programme that she has developed is being used by over thirty thousand groups throughout the USA. She asserts that people have to eat thin, which means picking at food and leaving most of it but, most importantly, they have to acknowledge that they are truly suffering from a spiritual hunger which they are confusing with a physical hunger. Stop running to the fridge and turn to God instead. Having examined from a feminist point of view in Chapter 1 why women eat and how female size is viewed, I may be tempted to translate 'spiritual hunger' as 'hunger for justice and equality', and then conclude that Shamblin may have some-thing valuable here. I think I will wait a while before I reach that conclusion. The first point that makes me stop in my tracks is the assertion by Shamblin that her programme can be used to over-come other forms of ungodly behaviour apart from eating, such as alcohol abuse, drug abuse, homosexuality and claims of wives to be on an equal footing with their husbands.[27] All these things show the depth to which people will go to change everything but themselves, she tells us, and all these sins can be overcome by turning to God alone. She and her followers do not believe that even the fundamentalist churches have been tough enough in their message and so she started a church of her own called the Remnant Fellowship.

The advice Shamblin gives is very practical, even recommend-ing the best way to eat food: for example, sort through the pile of crisps you have on your plate looking for those with the most salt on, eat one or two as you go and leave the rest. She is not at all concerned about food wastage, quoting Exodus for her justifica-tion (God turned stored food into maggots). In the book she writes, 'If it rots or is wasted – so what. He has more for you.'[28] Perhaps this more than anything illustrates not God's abundant love but the myopia of privilege and indeed arrogance. Shamblin does with her outspokenness allow us to see what is often at the heart of these religious diet programmes and it appears to be a total lack of concern for anyone outside their own narrow world. Of course the 'have it and leave it' mentality is to show the strength of faith, but in my view it simply shows the worst form of consumerist anti-Christian religion it is possible to conceive of. However, to hear Shamblin speak is to hear of a conversion experience, albeit one that took some time. God revealed the programme to her gradually, more in the manner of the Exodus from Egypt than the road to Damascus. She prayed for guidance at each step and slowly added more spirituality to a programme that had begun as a purely secular diet regime. Thus was born the Weigh Down Diet! Prayer has also allowed her to add jewellery products, bookmarks and CDs of her son Michael singing Christian pop to the Weigh Down industry.

Shamblin is very critical of the secular diet industry, seeing it as in the grip of Satan because, as she explains, when one is in it there is no requirement to take the mind off food and direct it to God. Counting calories, we are told, is the work of the devil. The Bible on the other hand provides a diet manual for us, the fatted calf proving that God approves of filet mignon, and low-carbohydrate diets being in her view blasphemous because Jesus said 'I am the bread of life', so we too should eat bread and lots of it. Looking to Leviticus she notes that there is a grain offering made of oil, flour and salt and she declares with glee, 'My that grain offering is very similar to our present day Frito!'[29] Shamblin does suggest that people eat in moderation, which is good, and she also notes that whereas the secular diet industry makes a great deal of money from diet foods, she has not yet branched out in this way, but she also says that the only exercise a person needs is getting on their knees to pray.

Shamblin entices people into the programme with the promise of holy romance. She tells the almost-all-female audiences that God is a handsome and charming, loving and rich husband – he is the hero they have all been dreaming of. There are a number of worrying things here, not least the total buying in to the hierarchical figure of the rich, handsome hero. To quote Audre Lorde's analysis again, here we see the master's tools set out before us. There is no questioning of social and economic hierarchies and the accepted assumption that women who become slender will have access to all these things, not just as a divine love affair, but also in their lives. We have already seen that this appears to be true, with slender women having easier access to the trappings of patriarchal hierarchy, including the rich husband. There is something very disturbing for my Christian heart in this celebration of the divine consumer husband. Shamblin tells us that she has a crush on the Father but on hearing these words I do not assume that we will be entering the world of Margery Kempe,[30] the medieval mystic, who through her sexual relationship with Father and Son turned the reality of her gendered narrow world on its head. Margery entered into a sensual relationship with the Godhead that consumed her and actually turned her from a woman of vainglory into a woman passionate for justice and female empowerment. I do not see that happening with Shamblin's romance with God. Shamblin says she takes this rich husband of hers on shopping trips because she likes to dress for him, but also because he has superb taste and is amazing at colour co-ordination. On her trips she asks if God likes her outfit and then she buys, and these are designer clothes because, as she says of God, 'He is fabulous, wonderfully good-looking. He is so powerful, so rich, so famous. He has got on designer clothes.'[31] One must not let the side down and so must dress accordingly. This appeals to Shamblin's audience of mainly middle-class white women of a certain age who also find themselves swooning along with her over their heart-throb God. This may be dieting for Jesus, but it is doing so in a very classy way with social advantage taken for granted in the rhetoric and assumed in the outcomes. The position of fashion accessory on the arm of God also extends to how Shamblin views the role of women, but there is a paradox here: Shamblin believes that women should not preach or carry a prophecy and so she is sad that there were no men to carry her Weigh Down message, and can only make theological sense of this as a sign of the end time. She takes as her guide on this the Book of Joel that says God will pour out his spirit on men and women alike in the last days.

Shamblin is not alone in her connecting the Jesus diet industry with the last days. On a website entitled 'No fatties in heaven'[32] we are told that it was the Tribulation (the last days) that made this Christian and would-be thin person understand God's demands that we be thin. When the Tribulation comes will he/she really be able to go hungry and enable others to eat? The real answer seemed to be no, and so this called for preparation in this life in order to face what will come – what was needed was a faith that would work in the face of starvation.[33] The way to this was desperate prayer, prayer of the addict who would have everything destroyed by the devil because of a desire to eat. The biblical comfort for this believer was the verse 'Woe unto you that are full now, for you shall hunger' (Luke 6:25), as it revealed that discipline was required now in order not to be left floundering at the Tribulation. In addition of course there are no fat people in heaven and no forgiveness for them either, it seems, because the fat have to remain fat for all eternity and watch the beautiful and the slim for that eternity, which would, it is assumed, be an eternal punishment. Weight loss also gives us a measuring stick by which to work out whether we are becoming disciplined people who deserve to survive the Tribulation at all. It is amazing that end-time thinking even affects the size of our hips! This form of thinking appears to be infecting the political right in the USA with potentially devastating global consequences. As we know there is a push in certain corners to enable and speed up a blood bath in the Middle East since those of an end-time tendency understand the setting up of Israel to be the beginning of the end in a very positive way. We must not forget that those who hold an end-time view actually welcome it and will indeed work through politics and religion to hasten its coming. Such people in power depend on the votes of the masses and, as we know, the electorate in the USA appears to be more concerned about a candidate's moral positions on certain issues than we appear to be in the UK. I do not really think it is too exaggerated to say that there are now thousands of women across the USA who are getting a diet of old-time/end-time religion along with their weigh-in and they will slide their reduced bodies into voting booths for many years to come. Whether we like to admit it or not, President Bush has acted of late under the influence of end-time thinking so that we do have an example of where that can take us. We also see that he has placed representatives in the United Nations and observers in the European Union who are actively attempting to subvert many of the gains of women and minority people – this too is end-time thinking. Religious fundamentalism is built on the backs of women who by divine decree are confined to the home to rear children and serve men, an agenda that is also lurking in the Weigh Down programmes and others where women are seen as responsible for the size and shape of all their family. It is no wonder, then, that this religious/political right is concerned about the United Nations and what it sees as its liberal policy-making,[34] which is to say its concern for the rights of women and children. The Christian Right believes that children's rights undermine parental authority and, for example, that the Convention for the Elimination of Discrimination against Women undermines and even destroys family life. They also wish to overturn any equality laws relating to homosexuality. We do not have to go very far to see this divisive thinking – we can see it in Shamblin's claim that her programme can be extended to other devil-inspired realities such as women seeking equality, and homosexuality. There are links here that may make us uncomfortable but that we would be unwise to ignore. End-time thinking, as unbiblical as so much of it is in the finer detail, is becoming a big political threat, and if we are to ingest it along with a consumer-driven crush on God then we need to ask some hard questions.

You shall be white as snow: we shall be rich

It is difficult not to totally dismiss Shamblin as a lunatic, because the way in which she speaks of the Bible, faith, the Trinity and the body are nothing short of laughable. What stops me laughing is the message of advanced capitalism that lurks beneath this holy foolery and, as always, keeping that in place, the gendered message of inequality. This is no laughing matter and really does deserve some theological response. Shamblin is not a theologian, but it seems increasingly these days that this does not matter: she has a received message and, strangely for a countercultural gospel, the message fits the dominant paradigm perfectly, with the occasional religious curio thrown in, such as biblical eating habits. I have for some time now been suggesting that the bodies of women within a countercultural incarnational religion are powerful sites of resistance to the worst excesses of patriarchy as practised through our economic and social systems, so such handing over of women as this programme makes possible fills me with horror as well as sadness. The radical gospel of equality that feminist theology has demonstrated to be close to the message of the early Jesus movement is nowhere to be seen here in gender, economics, class or (as we shall see) race. I almost dare to say Shamblin's Weigh Down group could be white supremacist simply because they are declaring a gospel of superior beauty and bearing which does exclude black people whether deliberately or not. They would, I think, counter this claim by the few black women who appear on websites testifying to their transformed lives through surrender to Jesus and the Weigh Down Diet. As we know from years of postcolonial study the discourse of whiteness goes deeper than this and even includes black people in its insidious projections.

Griffith is amongst the first to point out to us that beneath the facade of the normal and natural beautiful body lurk some very concerning assumptions about beauty itself. She writes that Christian diet cultures have a central role in 'the reproduction and naturalization of a racialized ideal of whiteness purged of the excesses associated with non-white cultures'.[35] Susan Bordo has researched this question from a secular viewpoint and been able to show that the practices of the western diet culture have normalised women in a worrying way that has led to the diminishment of cultural diversity in relation to the bodies of women. Her research indicates that men from whatever racial and economic background who were teenagers in the 1970s onwards are more likely to go for slender, flat-stomached, tight-bottomed women than they were previously estimated to do.[36] From the point of view of a Christian diet culture of the fundamentalist kind there are indeed alarm bells here since, as we know, Christian theology has been very white itself for some time, indeed white supremacist at times and in places. There has always been an assumption, spoken or unspoken, in Christian theology that God is white, and with the desire for colonial expansion the cross and the white man became almost inseparable. There has been a great deal of womanist theology on the subject as well as sound critiques from many parts of the world, so there is no need to rehearse them all here. What it is worth saying is that a white Christ was lurking behind it all, a Christ who could not value difference but rather had to be used to impose pre-conceived ideas of worth and with it hierarchy. This Christ, as I say, has been forcefully critiqued, and most mainstream theology is now at the very least aware of the necessity to be ever mindful of the way in which traditional theology with its notion of dualism can so easily be used in the service of divisive hierarchy. The old theological world let us live in an easily divided and safe world, good/bad, white/black, man/woman, literally in order of closeness to God, goodness, social acceptance and access. This was all based on an erroneous interpretation of incarnation that came to believe one had to rise above the flesh in order to live a life of the spirit, and that this was a pure life pleasing to God. There were barriers to this life and, as indicated, they were colour and gender, both of which were seen as existing in more dense matter and far less spirit. We are all familiar with the way in which this has affected women and of course we also know that this explicit narrowing of the incarnation reality deeply affected black nations too, especially when it was found that sub-Saharan Africans were the ones who survived the rigors of slavery the best.[37] Other races had been tried but had not been physically strong enough to survive – this unhappy fact led to the creation of an erroneous racist theology that looked for biblical justification for white authority and black servitude. The task was aided by the hierarchical dualism that had come into Christianity much earlier and continues to serve it badly.[38]

Of course there are still groups that actively advocate the division of the races and discrimination based on these arguments, but we have comforted ourselves that they are minority groups that do not have a great deal of influence. After all, we have seen the ills of apartheid and the violence and unrest that such systems generate, and we are not keen to go there. But have we ever really accepted the full message of diversity? Does equality simply mean access to the white system and the expectation that those so graced as to be included will in fact play the game by the right rules? The 'bleacher preachers' may not look as they once did, but it seems they are still there and one suspects that this time they are dressed in corporate suits. There is no doubt that the corporate slim image has a white face and that there is much money to be made from this image. Diversity requires much thought and a great deal of celebration of real difference if it is to be truly grounded in our world. There seems to be very little evidence that it has, and in the theological world the strict boundaries of the constructed Christ make it very difficult to move much beyond inclusion. We rarely if ever get to a place where difference and diversity affect our theological/christological frames.[39] On the odd occasion that they do, there is generally uproar and a putting to the margins of the offending challenge. We should, then, in many ways expect that the Christian diet industry would have a settled image of an assumed whiteness, since it most certainly has that of a white Christ. This is the Christ who was the backbone of segregation in the southern States in the USA where most of these Christian diet industries reside. I do not feel it is too exaggerated to ask if we can see a cultural influence here between the recently desegregated south, the religion that held segregation in place and the emergence of a diet culture that is based on a notion of perfect femaleness that consciously or unconsciously assumes this to manifest as white. The perfect Southern lady can be seen in Gwen Shamblin with her piled-up hair, Gucci taste and $3.2 million anti-bellum mansion in Nashville – and she is not alone in this representation of the perfect woman for God.

Right from the early days of the Christian diet literature examples of the 'coloured' woman were used to show that indeed this was not 'for them' since they could not really understand what was being suggested. The 'otherness' of non-white and also non-middle-class women was used to illustrate the elect nature of those who could and should adopt the diet culture. It is spelt out very clearly by Anne Ortlund in her book *Disciplines of the Beautiful Woman* (1984). In this classic work of white supremacy she states that 'primitives' are not expected to be slim – they are 'plump and dark' and she has witnessed it herself. She writes, 'I have bent down and stooped into a thatched hut deep in the jungles of South America and seen a cotton print dress hanging inside, the joy of that little primitive pudding-bag-shaped woman. Someone will have parted with it and through missionaries bearing the love of Jesus, it came to her.'[40] 'And what else came to her?' I find myself yelling at the page. Just how embedded this toxic rhetoric of supremacy is within certain kinds of

Christianity is, I think, made very clear by Ortlund's utterances, and although many of the Jesus dieters today would not be so obvious, and indeed may be surprised when told they too were peddling a white supremacist agenda, it is still there to see. They may be tempted to defend themselves by saying they are writing for a white audience, and that it is because of the historic African American lack of concern for matters of size that their community has not stigmatized the large in the same way that the white society has done. This, however, would in my view only be half a defence, which fails to acknowledge the ideology of thinness that is linked to that of civilisation and breeding.

There are those who would argue that being thin is open to all, so that spreading a gospel of thinness, just like spreading 'education', is an excellent Christian witness to the world – it is open to all and makes the world accessible to all. And the flaw is? Well, where is the real democracy, where is the valuing of diversity and different cultural norms? We have long ago been alerted to the questionable virtues of universal education and perhaps we need to wake up quickly to the devastating possibilities ahead if we export to all cultures and racial groups a gospel of thinness. Marcella Althaus-Reid[41] has introduced us to the concept of decency that was exported along with the Conquistadors to Latin America and she has illustrated the truly devastating results of this in the private lives of the women who came under its scrutiny; they were transformed from embodied women who had self-esteem into the disobedient and never-good-enough daughters of Eve. In short, they were judged by a foreign set of sexual mores which under occupation they could never fulfil, even had they wished to, and against which they were always to be judged as the primitive other. This prejudice was theological in origin and in turn affected theology and the way in which Christ became represented. The universal gospel of thinness carries with it not decency but civilisation and breeding, it carries the un-spoken but assumed gospel of advanced capitalism and the open road that such a way of life is believed to give. All this in the name of Jesus – the irony does not need to be spoken. What does need to be examined, and I will do so in the final chapter, is the way in which this corporate body of controlled thinness is affecting the Christ who is preached and how an indecent Christ may be the theological starting point for a Fat Jesus.

It has to be acknowledged that to be thin and fit takes time and money and this too raises some deeply disturbing and complex questions that within the American context are also racial in nature. The polls on weight show that African American and Hispanic women are considerably more overweight than white women and on closer analysis this appears to be linked to educational and economic factors.[42] So what are we saying here? Is it the more educated and economically better off who have given in to the white rhetoric and have the means to achieve it? After all, good quality food costs much more than junk food or a supermarket's own products. Or is it that better education opens one's eyes to a self-evident truth, that it is blessed to be thin? Certainly, as we have seen, if that blessing is believed to come through job prospects and upwardly mobile marriage then it is indeed blessed to be thin. It is very difficult to decide on an answer, but what we do see is that Christian diet literature does not spare a thought for matters of educational and economic difference, the assumption throughout being middle class as well as white. This has led commentators like bell hooks[43] to question whether it is in the American national interest to include black people in this rhetoric, because it may be that society functions best when there are physically unwell outsiders too, those who are never fit enough to challenge the basic inequalities of a patriarchal society. Good health is a white privilege! American Christianity has from the beginning been affected by questions of race and whiteness and they are bound to be here in this discourse too. It is a matter of debate what one does when they are spotted.

This chapter has shown how the discourse of women and food has changed under a Protestant theology through the late nineteenth to early twenty-first century. We saw with Sarah Jacob the beginnings of an economic gain in matters of food restriction for women, and we have witnessed this turning into multi-million-dollar industries. Sarah Jacob lived at a time of great change for women and it has been argued that this was significant in matters of women's eating habits. The purely religious explanations for such behaviour were waning and the psychological were gaining ground. This meant that the internal world of the fasting saint became the external world of the patient, the one who had an eating disorder and thus a complex psychology that fuelled it. In a sense what was happening was the privatising of the bodily actions of women and with this move it can be argued that the political meaning of such actions were ring-fenced and silenced. This radical bodily engagement was reduced to an internally disordered psyche and the discourse became studied but no longer challenging – this was simply another strange thing that women did.

As we have seen, the religious dimension behind food consumption did not totally die away and it does seem to have been part of the background for the new emergence of religious food restriction. It is interesting to see how food itself was viewed as having moral qualities, with distinctions made between good and bad food, which still persist today even in the secular food industry, and which seemed to be absent from the medieval view of food. Another noticeable difference is that many of the starving saints talked of feeding the poor – indeed they did themselves feed the poor, while we have the likes of Gwen Shamblin appearing to be oblivious to the plight of the hungry worldwide. Her philosophy of waste 'because God will provide more' is hard to fathom unless we see it in a theological frame that is only concerned with personal salvation, in short an ultra-Protestant obsession with self.

The new Christian diets are meant to carry a truly democratic lifestyle that would appeal to North American sensibilities and ideas deeply embedded about their country and its truly open mentality. We all have bodies and with the right amount of willpower we can all be thin. In reality we have seen that the Christian diet industry is profoundly class- and racially infected. Through its rhetoric fat people have become excluded, eroticised and made primitive, all of which symbolises filth and ungodliness, all perfectly in keeping with a message that believes eternal salvation hinges on it. The Christian diet industry is dealing with the weight of a sinful world which appears to manifest as poor and black more often than anything else! The moral rhetoric about fat people has become embedded in fundamentalist theology which as we have seen in its Southern manifestations is already prone to racism because of its divisive dualistic underpinning that has never been tempered by liberal theological rhetoric. The so-called democratising potential of the Christian diet industry is in reality another form of colonialism: it peddles an idea of beauty that is white all the way to its polished and manicured fingernails. As with so many 'good ideas', I believe we have to be careful before we ingest its rhetoric because we literally will be embodying our own oppression. There is no diversity in this model as indeed there has not been in such ideas as the universal Christ who lives and breathes in metaphysical absolutes, and it is this Christ who has been overcome through calls for justice and equality. He may now be masquerading as a slim, white, affluent Christian woman but he still needs rooting out. It is also worth mentioning at this stage that this model is also heterosexual. Studies show that lesbians have to date been less affected by diet cultures than their heterosexual sisters and, whatever the positive reasons for this, no doubt it will be seen by those in the Jesus diet camp as just another ungodly rebellion. The Christian diet culture assumes and one could even suggest promotes a vanilla/girlie form of heterosexuality, and where it does deal with men there is a lord-and-master rhetoric. The men need to be slim in order to best discharge their manly duties of taking care of their families through hard work. Further, their fasting can turn them into 'fortresses of flesh that protects the woman you love', [44] a reinstatement of the phallic God if ever I heard one. This is not at all surprising, given the type of theology that underpins these programmes and, as we have seen, Shamblin even believes that her diet programme can help correct other forms of deviance such as homosexuality and the desire of women to be equal with their husbands. The old binaries are in place in her system and they carry with them the hierarchical realities. Dangerously these are now linked with right-wing politics as never before and the new control in the home is mirrored by a new desire for social control – the same men who fast to be fortresses at home also fast to aid US foreign policy in its colonial enterprise.[45]

In the light of this perhaps I should not find the consumer capitalism that is embedded in many of these programmes as truly disturbing as I do – after all, global markets are what the right wing want. God is turned into an 'ultimate shopper' with great taste so that he becomes the heavenly fashion consultant.

His pockets are deep, he will provide you with the funds to be beautiful, so that his name may be praised. What kind of Christ is emerging here, and should we be too surprised? Perhaps we should not, because this is really only an extension of the God who sees disability as sin and is therefore one of the beautiful people. We see before us the very God and Christ that liberation theology has unmasked as unjust and exploitative. It is as though the last forty years of experiential theology never existed. Perhaps worryingly, there is an experiential element lurking here, but it is the kind that never gets beyond what is good for the individual. The modern Christian diet rhetoric has moved on from notions of health based in good and bad food to the idea of prosperity – it is rare to read in the literature that one diets and gets healthy full stop. This health, and beauty, is not only the key to eternal salvation but also to a very good life here. There are echoes of the True Love Waits campaign which has much the same theological underpinning and certainly sets out the same results: salvation and a wealthy husband and success in this life. This campaign speaks in terms of the price on women's virginity and this language is not metaphorical.[46] The women in both scenarios seem to be making themselves bait for advanced capitalists; worse still, they also seem to be the motivating factor behind the men's drive for wealth and esteem. I really do not see what they would call gospel values in this at all and certainly the only Kingdom it can lead to is one with very tight boundaries and narrow entrances since only the slim elite can enter.

The bodies of women, and some men, are being used in just the way Mary Douglas tells us they are – to create a bounded identity for a group, in this case the saved. But of course what is also happening is the creation of the body of Christ and this Christ is being projected onto the world through the practices of the believers. In asking what this Christ looks like, the modern day theologian is not even asking if such a Christ actually ultimately exists, but rather what are the lived consequences of a Christ imaged in such a way? For feminist liberation theology Christ is always ethical rather than an abstract set of metaphysics. What world emerges if we lived 'as if' this diet Christ called us to do his will? A very narrow one, devoid of the glorious rainbow of incarnational diversity and divine potential that is our birthright; a very politically aggressive one, attempting to project the pale face of vanilla womanhood onto a global screen for the economic advantages that such a projection ensures. Perhaps after all this incarnational theologian does not have to despair totally because, as Foucault tells us, where there is power there is also resistance and so, sisters, will you Slim for Him or bake cakes for the Queen of Heaven? There is a lot resting on your answer!

Chapter Four

Women and desire: cream cakes, champagne and orgasms

As long as we fear the emotional power of the hag we will direct our attention and interests to appearances rather than to pleasure and enjoyment.[1]

In this chapter I want to look at the question of women and desire and how this particularly links with food and the way in which women eat or do not eat. We have seen how in various ways women are removed from their bodies and consequently from their deepest desires. These desires are taken over by society and moulded to fit what best suits the overarching patriarchal model. Women then come to fear their inner strength, which is the seat of their desires, and begin to find a superficial level of worth through a false posturing in their bodies, a posturing that fits the social order in all its personal and political complexity. Not all women are able to do this in a way that goes unnoticed and, like any other deep-felt rebellion, this rebellion of women sits on their bones.

Anorexia is actually a misleading term since it implies that women have no appetite, whereas the reality is that they have one and act to suppress and overcome it. We are also being mis-led if we think that the majority of overweight women do not know that they are full. So what are we looking at here in our western culture? The underweight and the overweight – do they have anything in common? The short answer is yes, they are all women living within a heteropatriarchal reality, a reality that does not give them much room to breathe. Further they have, like so many others in different ways, chosen to live their rebellion on their bodily frames. As women have gained more intellectual and economic power patriarchal society has found more and more ways to reinforce female inferiority and since women are meant to display their bodies more than men this has been a prime site for that game to be played out. The notion of the ideal female body is one that is 'a manifestation of misogynist norms flowing from a culture where women are devalued and disempowered'.[2] The bodies of women are meant to regulate themselves if the full power of society is to be acted out on them. Perhaps, then, what we are seeing in both overweight and underweight women is an attempt to take that power for themselves, to live their own desires in their own skins. Of course given the regulatory power of the bigger picture these rebellions can often seem self-destructive. But if we are not to lose the political implication we have to realise that there is something very wrong with a society in which the tyranny of slenderness means that many women – the estimate is some 70 per cent – have one difficulty or another with eating. One in five of these women has such difficulty with our society that she has an eating disorder. This takes hold very young as we have seen, with 78 per cent of young women believing they are overweight by the age of thirteen; this bears little resemblance to what weight they actually are.

This system does not just 'exist': it is held in place by a number of strategies that disable women, ranging from the language we use about female bodies to the way in which we treat them in everything from public acts to the smallest acts of intimacy and care-giving. Studies have shown, for example, that mothers feed girl children less than their boys. Nevertheless these assumptions are played out on the bodies of girls from day one and are bound to have some effect. It has been suggested that the limited calorific intake and the shorter time it takes to feed the child will lay the foundations of a sense of undernourishment and under-nurturing that will set up patterns for the future.[3] Hartley suggests these patterns may involve eating disorders while others like Wolf believe that the significance of this goes much deeper. She understands that food has always been viewed as a symbol of social worth through the generations and across cultures. It has been one way in which we honour the members of our societies. The breaking of bread together has always been one way to signal allies and equals, and as long as women and girls are getting the message that they do not warrant as much then they also get the message that they are not equals in society.[4]

There is a further message implicit in this early restriction of food, that self-denial is at the heart of being a woman. I have written extensively about how this affects women's sexuality but it also affects their relationship to food and their self-perception in terms of their role as nurturer. In short, women are groomed to be nurturers and not to expect nurture. Following on from Wolf's point we never really expect to be the honoured and equal guests at the table but rather to ensure that the table is full with all that will make the guests feel honoured. Perhaps we should take a leaf out of Samoan women's books: they exaggerate what they eat, because of their very honoured place in society; women are thought well of when they are big and interestingly there are very low levels of the illnesses we in western society associate with weight gain. Whatever culture we are in, we find ourselves in unequal power relations searching for our place and meaning, and we tend as embodied individuals to act that out through the body, which is after all where we live. From a feminist liberation perspective we need to be careful that the meaning we are seeking is not simply found in the existing structures. In looking for our place we need to be ever mindful of the countercultural potential of the tradition we follow, that of Christian incarnation. Incarnation, as we know, is extremely embodied at the same time as challenging all the boundaries of what it is we routinely understand as embodied reality.

The Christian god/man does not have a fixed nature, even though subsequent theology has argued that he does, but a permeable and unstable nature. The stories relate to us the many changes that took place within and around the body of Christ which highlighted the unstable categories involved in God incarnate. It is through changes from divine to flesh, flesh and blood to bread and wine and from human to cosmic spirit that the full incarnation of redemptive praxis takes place. Each of these, fully understood, signal a change in place, in position and in power relation; as such they are useful resources for those of us who are playing with our own embodiment in order to live our full incarnate birthright.

The Christian story is one of God dwelling in flesh, which shatters all our myopic earthbound ideas and makes them subject to change. The dynamic life force which is the divine erupts in diversity and the energy of it will not be inhibited by laws and statutes, shapes and sizes. Far from creating the same yesterday, today and tomorrow, this dynamism is always propelling us forward into new curiosities and challenges. It does not shut us off from the world; it is the world drawing us into more of ourselves as we spiral in the human/divine dance. It is this becoming more of ourselves that is so difficult for women when we are regulated in our bodies from so young. However, incarnation demands that we seek performances that disrupt the status quo rather than bolsters it. This means in the world we live in that we have to find ways to challenge the structures that bind us and in this context that means the stories told about women and size.

Say it, sisters: big and bold!

Part of this countercultural living can begin with how we speak about our bodies. Monique Wittig tells us that language is not merely words but rather a set of acts repeated over time that produce reality, a reality that will eventually be seen as fact. So effective is this that the impression is given that the reality spoken is somehow pre-social and pre-discursive, or, to put it in the language of theology, it appears to be the pre-existent will of God. As we saw with the Slim for Him programmes this was the reality of slender bodies: they were pre-existent with God – indeed for Shamblin God's body was also this model of slender beauty. Wittig says that 'language casts sheaves of reality upon the social body and these sheaves are not easily discarded ... they violently stamp and shape it'.[5] Their oppressive power also goes deep as the structure of language coerces people to participate in the very language of their own oppression. In other words there appears to be no other way to speak, as it is assumed that those negatively framed by language, in this case fat women, are unintelligible and that for them there is no possibility of being a speaking subject. Wittig is aware that the power of language is enormous because it also shapes concepts, categories and science and, once this occurs, 'there is nothing abstract about the power that sciences and theories have to act materially and actually upon our bodies and minds, even if the discourse that produces it is abstract ... All the oppressed know this power and have to deal with it.'[6]

Wittig is aware that while the power of language can oppress it is also the way beyond oppression because it is not magical nor set in stone. Language indeed is very 'plastic'; it can be a criminal act but it can also be a revolutionary act. As she sees it the practical task for women is to establish subjectivity through speaking, which will enable them to cast off the speech patterns that deform them or turn them into relative beings. It is true that Wittig is speaking about women and gender when she says what she does about language, but it seems to me the same is also true about the shape and size of women, not simply the state of being female. It is urgent, then, that we use different language so that these alternative speech acts become embedded as fact, but as facts based on our perception of our bodies, not the perceptions of the male gaze and other vehicles of patriarchal order. In other words we need to talk ourselves into a subject position; to talk ourselves into the real world.

How this power of language actually works in Christianity is immediately evident when we look at the scriptures because it is through speaking and naming that the Christian and Jewish God created the world (Genesis 1). This fondness for speech and its power is further developed in the Christian scriptures with 'the Word' believed to be at the beginning of creation and actually being God (John 1:1). Words, then, within the Christian tradition are believed to have the power to create human reality; to shape our world. What is said and who says it becomes a matter of huge significance theologically as well as socially.

This power of naming has been acknowledged as crucial by feminists since it not only expresses and shapes our experience but also gives us the power to transform our reality. We are rather tired of the story of how Adam, the man, names the woman and the rest of creation; we have not found this as liberating as the gospels proclaim our lives should be. We wish to find new language and to therefore live in new worlds, worlds created by our divine speech. Language is important in feminist theology because it clearly shows us how we are perceived in the world and in theology. For many of us this is the first step to anger, the anger that Harrison and others tell us is the first step to finding self-worth since it signals that a wrong has been done. It is then a righteous anger and one that women have traditionally found difficult to own. When language is shaped by our lived realities it also enables us to 'hear each other to speech'; it is a way through the silence of our experience, the deadening blanking of what it really is like to be embodied as a female under patriarchy. We have seen how our bodies have been shaped by the words of others and now we must begin to shape *our* bodies with *our* words.

Amongst feminist theologians Mary Daly stands out as having been most creative with language. She reclaims words from patriarchy and invents words when she feels that women's experience is beyond patriarchal language. She says that as a gynocentric writer she wants to give rise to intuitive play in our own space which enables thinking which is vigorous, informed, multi-dimensional, independent, creative and tough. Daly plays with words and invites us to hear them again in a new way; a way that throws light on our experience as women. She takes words that have traditionally conveyed negative images of women and transforms them. 'Spinsters' are no longer unmarried women with the images that conveys, but women spinning webs of wonder and unfolding the future. Hags, crones, witches are all 'wanderlusting women' who wander through patriarchy wielding labryses, 'double axes of our own wild wisdom and wit, which cut through the mazes of man-made mystification, breaking the mind bindings of master-minded doublethink.'[7] Daly takes the sting out of language that has been designed to control women and she replaces it with the desire to spark and spin. What would language look like if we did this about our embodied realities, if women of all shapes and sizes called themselves beautiful and meant it? In a sense we have a biblical mandate for this, as we are told that we are beautifully and awesomely made and there is no weight and size chart attached. What if we insisted on being treated as beautiful regardless of how we measure up to the expected norms of society? The answer is plain: we would embed in society repeated speech acts that would in time become reality, would in time become facts. Do we have the self-esteem to exert that much pressure on language, one of the pillars of our society?

To find this self-esteem is very difficult in a society that constantly invades us with negativity. The fat female body, for example, is invaded with comments and bombarded with pathologised hatred and fear.[8] This is because fat women do not play by the rules and so in this way they embody a threat, a space-taking threat at that. They have bodies that occupy space in a way that violates the rules of sexual politics and of body movement; they do not confine themselves to the meagre space allowed women in the public arena, and they have muscles and so do not fall down under their own weight. This is not as it should be: this is countercultural and has to be punished, which it is through language and through attempted social exclusion, as we have seen. There is too much flesh for a society based in Christian dualism to cope with, but we could argue that the fat body is demanding that society finds a new vision of embodiment that is no longer disdainful of the flesh, and that theology thinks again about how it engages with the realities of incarnation and the divine potential therein. Fat bodies are never portrayed as effective, powerful or sexual, let alone as divine, and in this way there is a strange paradox at work: those bodies which should be most visible because of their size are erased through our cultural perceptions. It is an irony that bodies that have curves and fleshy buttocks, hips and breasts are not viewed as sexual or eroticised in our society, while those that have lost their secondary sexual characteristics through dieting are projected as paragons of female sexuality. But is it really so peculiar in a society that does not value women? After all, the glamorisation of the artificially created female that actually erases real women is in keeping with such a culture! The erasure goes deep because those who starve themselves to meet the ideal actually affect their internal as well as external femaleness; ovulation and menstruation are affected when the tyranny of slenderness cuts too deep into their flesh. And here we hit another point of countercultural speaking/ knowing: fat bodies store more oestrogen which heightens sexuality. This has led researchers to investigate whether this can possibly be true as it goes against the truth spoken through the male gaze, which declares the fat body to be asexual or even desexualised. Research has shown that women with more body fat do want more sex, which appears to be flying in the face of the cultural norms of white western society where the desired sex object in fact appears to be less interested than the abhorrent object.

Of course this inability to speak goes deep if we are to believe some body theorists. Helena Mitchie[9] amongst others theorises female hunger in terms of unspeakable desires for sex and power. She illustrates how this was clear to see in Victorian times when women had restrictions placed on their public eating that directly paralleled their restricted sexual construction and of course their public power. But why should they be unspeakable today when we believe that women are more equal in the discourse at least in the areas of sex and power in the personal and public realms? The answer at the theoretical level is that women are clearly not feeling fulfilled in these areas and, in addition, seem still to lack the self-esteem or self-worth to insist upon such satisfaction. Shamblin and her followers, as we saw, insisted that God fills the spiritual hunger, but there was a cost as I perceived it: all should know their place, and this was a rather traditional place with men in charge and women glad of it. This would admittedly help in the area of women wishing to have recognition, which may be seen as power – they can be recognised as good Christian wives and mothers who have no need for any further esteem. I would argue then that they do not in fact have a great deal of self-worth since their worth appears to hinge on their ability to fulfil a preconceived ideal in the service of others. I have addressed elsewhere the sexual reality for many of these women[10] and so will not repeat the argument but it is the case that abuse is very frequent in such fundamentalist homes, so the issue of female desire and satisfaction in this area is not high on the agenda.

The splitting off in the body that is required to allow women to live under the oppressive sexual regimes that they do is also the kind that works well in relation to the denial of their sense of worth and the way in which they will punish their bodies in order to regulate size. However, Chernin[11] tells us that women attempting to regulate their hunger and appetites can fill them with despair because these are deeply rooted in sensuality. Attempting to regulate hunger is the same as denying one's sexual needs, something women are encouraged to do but find that it has a price, since it is an expression of who each woman is. Food, she argues, is giving oneself and others permission to enjoy the sensual aspects of the self. This is not something that our western culture under the influence of Christianity and latterly under the crushing weight of advanced capitalism has been very good at enabling. The former because it flies in the face of the fundamental dualistic split at the heart of much Christian thinking and the latter because such satisfaction does not fuel the capitalist treadmill. What is needed is quick short-lived fixes and bodies that do not nurture themselves well but rather labour for what is in the future. Anorexia, as we have seen, is a condition that is based in denial and a splitting of the self, body and mind. It has also been suggested that those who are overweight also distance themselves in the same way from the demanding gaze of patriarchy. Chernin, however, insists that our bodies will express even the feelings that we disown, and she encourages us to understand our bodies as objects of glory which contain wisdom and wonders. She urges us to give respect to our flesh and take instruction from it,[12] and delights in the wisdom of the menopausal body which she understands as the rounding out of our lives and the broadening of our experience being made manifest on our bones. Patriarchal society attempts to control this manifestation and in doing so it is attempting, not for the first time, to control nature. Women need to rebel against this and glory in the wisdom of their flesh. It has been very difficult for women to do this because the female body with its intimate connection with life and death and its evidently changing character has, within the Christian tradition, been viewed as the furthest from the unchanging God of metaphysical absolutes. This changeability of women has made them appear far too bodily for the Christian tradition to cope well with, and Chernin would argue that this has translated into secular man's inability to cope with his own mortality. She goes on to say, 'If men could tolerate this they might also be willing to let women grow large, become mature and carry in pride the natural wonder of the human body in all its abundance.'[13] This inability has also meant that men retreat from grown women as erotic images and look for safety in the relatively unchanging fixed image of the childlike body. They find safety in this vulnerability in a way that they can not in the fully grown body of a woman because there is something deeply disturbing to them in that mature flesh. What is it, and may this dis-ease of men be the origin of their scapegoating of women and the origin of women's denial of their own desires?

Coping with maternal fleshiness

There is a large amount of speculation in this area but amongst the most persuasive and academically credible theorists is Dorothy Dinnerstein, who has suggested that the inevitable loss of the primary love, the mother, is the most basic human grief felt in all genders and is compensated for in an array of healthy and unhealthy activities throughout our lives. Chernin puts it this way: 'Woman's body our first home. Our first knowledge of unfathomable mysteries. The first cause of our innocent suffering when it casts us out of itself.'[14] If this is the case then theology and religious practice has a place here making visible the grief and healing the wounds, so that we may all live fuller and less destructive lives – more abundant, more fully incarnate. Lives that are not dictated to by negative projections based in psychological pain. The problem is that the loss is experienced differently by boys and girls leading to a desire for distinct compensations all played out in a gendered and heavily patriarchal world. This will have its say on size as well as sexuality.

Both men and women wish to experience again the nurture that was evident in the primal love, but in a patriarchal world this is extremely difficult. For men it is a lot easier both physically and psychologically: a woman's body is like that of the mother, so just being close will enable men to recreate the closeness of the early years and awaken memories of infant–mother bliss. For men, then, intercourse will satisfy their need for nurturance, but this is not the case for women. After all, merely being close to a man will not remind a woman of her mother's body. In addition, she is cast into the mother role by being the one to provide bodily pleasure. We have seen how this influences the way in which women are encouraged to view their bodies and the way in which men have exerted their power in society to shape the bodies of women according to external circumstances. For example, as we have already seen, Sophia Loren combined sensuality with nurture at an historical moment when men had been facing death and hardship on a daily basis and so combined their desire for sex with an exaggerated desire for nurture. The female body has then to bear the weight of the male psychological as well as physical need for fulfilment. The exchange of pleasure that would signal a mature relationship is often absent within this psychological construction that has become known as heteropatriarchy.[15] As a woman cannot, usually, penetrate a man the emotional merging signalled by such an activity is difficult without vicarious merging. It is this vicarious merging that is so dangerous for women who through their capacity to give nurturance and care lose their autonomy. Men, under patriarchy, are able to find nurture and remain autonomous while women's capacity to love will often lead to a life of emotional pain and a yearning for idealised love, as well as frustration when this is not attained.[16] In short her desires are not named and certainly not fulfilled when this is the frame within which she acts out her need to heal the rupture of mother love and bliss.

If we simply read Dinnerstein at face value we would be looking at a world where the bodies of women bear the consequences of an unfortunate system that has developed, based in the pain and suffering of both sexes brought about by moving from the mother. Men, it is assumed, will bear the cost in other ways as I am sure they do. However, not all theorists are as measured in their analysis of the situation. Deliberately using the language of postcolonial discourse, Haunani-Kay Trask brings home forcibly the situation of women within patriarchally defined institutions, including what may be called body politics. She says, 'Our bodies have been taken from us, mined for their natural resources (sex and children) and deliberately mystified. Five thousand years of Judeo-Christian tradition, virulent in misogyny, have helped enforce the idea that women are 'unclean" ... our ignorance about our own primary terrain – our bodies – is in the self interest of patriarchy.'[17] So what may start as a common human condition seeking solutions has become a ground for gender politics and the inevitable embodied consequences that such politics always gives rise to.

While Trask describes the problem she is also keen to create an alternative, and for her this too lies in two paths, the return to the mother and the return to the body. Both are necessary because in both are at the roots of patriarchy, and the denial of the female erotic/desire that this heralds. Within the Christian tradition this return to the mother is diminished, as the female aspect of deity has been all but obliterated except for faint glimpses through the construction of Mary, who, as she is conveyed, is the perfect object of mother bliss for the pining sons, and the impossible role model of virgin mother for women. The return to the mother helps us look again at and analyse 'how we dwelt in two worlds, the daughters and the mothers in the kingdom of the sons',[18] and having looked, to re-image how this may be one world of female empowerment and sisterhood. Chernin believes that as we grow and enter the world of the fathers even the sons become nervous and so they too wish to return to the body of a woman for their security. As they grow, this return takes on an added dimension of control, which is the only way to ensure that they receive comfort as they wish it; the control eliminates anxiety that is there because of the primal memory of the withdrawal of the mother's body. Chernin claims that this is projected into a social system that keeps women helpless. She further observes that the slender or even anorexic body helps men feel more secure since it is a body purged of all the power to conjure up memories of the past, all that could remind them of women's mysterious power[19] and the pain that the withdrawal of that lush first world inflicted on them. Lelwica has an interesting take on this too: she says that childlike bodies are less threatening to men particularly since the Women's Movement, which has called for power for women in the world not just in the home. However, she also sees the Women's Movement as having a profound affect on the bodies of women in a way we may not have expected. She argues that for some women the obsession with thinness reflects an attempt to balance the selfless, nurturing and caring for others with the independence, self-reliance and public success that women are now able to achieve.[20]

However, the search is on, as Trask claims, for courageous mothering that does not encourage daughters to fall into the self-sacrificial mode required by sons and patriarchy but rather a love that, while nurturing, is a process of women giving birth to themselves, a kind of psychic midwifery for women's transformation.[21] The love that is sought is then philosophical as well as psychological and emotional; it is a conscious befriending of the female and a nurturing of that femaleness to autonomy. The nurturing of this autonomy in a world that dictates the patriarchal law that only men inherit the love of women, and that women have to be taught this, is deeply threatening to patriarchy – this is the feminist eros. It may be here that the issue of women and size can find a starting point for rebellion when young women no longer allow themselves to become scapegoats for male anxiety and then, by projection, for culture's pain and inadequacy. Is it here that women find the self-love to deflect the rage that men can feel towards women, rather than sharing in it?

In a very uncharacteristic turn for a secular work, Trask engages with Robin Morgan when she names this kind of nurturing and empowering as love, and the body that enables it, sacramental – an anti-Christian sacrament. After a eucharistic celebration of the mother's body as the true bread and wine, Morgan goes on:

> Blessed be my brain
>> that I may conceive of my own power.
> Blessed be my breast
>> that I may give sustenance to those I love.
> Blessed be my womb
>> that I may create what I choose to create.[22]

The power of the external male Christ who, as we have seen, is the one behind much of the body-denying theology that has laid the foundations not only for Slim for Him but also for a secular society that functions in a dualistic manner, is replaced here by female flesh and blood, in women's real experience. The sacramental force of this is emphasised in order to challenge the denigration of the female body, and for the present purpose it also gives power to the role of nurturer. After all, the table we are invited to as Christians is the one that holds the Messianic Banquet and so the Christ that presides in female flesh is a fleshy Christ indeed.

This return to the mother that Trask advises is linked to a return to the body which may seem a foolish step to some, since women have been linked to the body for centuries in a negative and less than empowering way. However, as we have seen, the erotic is an activity of the mind and not just the body, and is the way in which we may have the greatest revolution, to claim back what has for so long been taken away and used against us is a tremendous challenge to the dominant system. As Trask puts it, 'The return to the mother and the return to the body are consciously taken journeys destined to weaken the power of the sexual under-structure and to make vivid the re-experiencing of instinctual gratification. In turn, these journeys enable the projection of an emancipated society: the feminist eros.'[23]

Trask takes the debate on a step by suggesting that one crucial area is a return to the mother, which is a real attempt to reclaim women's bodies from the discourse of dominance and submission right at the beginning – mothers not delivering their daughters to the kingdom of the sons, but rather feeding them with the power of their own flesh and wills. This mothering that she speaks of is not simply physical and is urgently needed between women who are friends and lovers. It may just be one way in which we overcome the male ambivalence towards the female body that we too have shared, making us less than powerful in our own skins and therefore open to external pressure and oppression.

Although Trask understands that there are dangers in a return to the mother and a return to the body, she is willing to take the risk and she urges others to do the same. Amongst the things she is asking us to face is the realm of the original mother, the devouring woman, as she has been seen in much psychological literature. Our mothers are first known to us through our hunger and it is commonly held that we attribute to them what we ourselves then felt, that is the desire to eat, swallow, suck. So we imagine that this huge female body that we find ourselves next to wants to eat us. On the reverse side of the coin we also know that if this body does not feed us we die, and this is an extremely precarious position for the young to be in. It is also the place where blame begins because we either have too much or not enough and 'this is the heartland of our obsession',[24] the place where we can be lost for ever if the breast we want is not there. The preoccupation with the female body, it is argued, is rooted in this primal experience because a woman's body is our world, 'a teeming and luxurious paradise in which woman is the universe',[25] a world in which taste, smell, touch and sight are all mixed and the internal and external are not clearly defined. It is argued that once men and women can overcome the instinct to blame and, for the male, the instinct to control all that raises fear in him, then the power of the erotic can be truly savoured and women can be connected with all their power and subjectivity. We have, on the whole, a long way to go!

Gendering the flesh

Male domination and with it the denial of desire in women works through the hegemony of impersonal organisation and the bodies of both women and society at large have been impersonally organised by aesthetics and rationality, two aspects better suited to Greek metaphysics than the sensual engagement of the divine with the world through the materiality of incarnation. Jessica Benjamin is very persuasive when she gives us some insight into how this works through the organisation of gender. Like many before her she acknowledges that masculinity and femininity are based on very different assumed principles and experiences and not just biological difference. Boys, she argues, lay the basis for the supremacy of the cold, impersonal nature of rationality from birth. They are not their mother, so their maleness is defined by discontinuity, which leads them to objectify her as an object, instrument of pleasure but not an independent person. This Benjamin sees as the very base of the lack of equality within the hetero system, which she understands as sexual but also political. Erotic domination, she says, is male anxiety about the relation to the mother which manifests in power over and denigration.[26] In this association of women with desexualised mother object the woman is stripped of agency in desire and viewed as empty, that is of having no autonomy or meaning beyond that which will be found when she is penetrated by the phallus which is the counterbalance to the fear of being engulfed and devoured by the maternal. This is where the question of size too plays a part: being engulfed by the mother is less likely as a psychological possibility if the body one is alongside is very childlike, a waif that does not carry the maturity of an adult female.

The phallus becomes the instrument of autonomy for men, the representation of freedom from the dependency on the powerful mother. However, it must not connect them with an object that they can not control since this may call into question the autonomy that is so crucial to their sense of self. For women this is entirely different, while they have no object with which to overcome this phallic monopoly.[27] This is why it is so important that women do not further cripple themselves through a removal from the reality of their bodies, and that they do not play the size game, which is a part of playing the game of male superiority. It is also making the body once more unrecognised and therefore less than useless in a woman's quest for desire. If we are to create new ways of being then we have to learn to tell the truth about our desires, which enable us to embody powerful ways of being female in the world. This lack of recognition which Benjamin associates with the male child's relationship with the mother and as the base of heteropatriarchal relationships has to be overcome through the prioritising of the female body, anatomically and symbolically, in our theological worlds. Benjamin says an understanding of desire as a need for recognition changes our view of the erotic experience: 'It enables us to describe a mode of representing desire unique to intersubjectivity which, in turn, offers a new perspective on women's desire.'[28] For her this intersubjectivity is spatial, it gives women room to grow, to be, and is not confined. Following Winnicott's insights she argues that the relationship between the self and others is spatial, it is a space that holds and a space that allows us to create.[29] It is this space that is denied women through the rigid boundaries of hetero reality, but it is the space that is crucial for the emergence of our interior self. This internal space will also, I wish to argue, make us more comfortable with taking more external space, which in the present world is viewed as a heresy.

Benjamin examines how this initial arrangement is worked out in society through the separation of the public and private spheres. This she sees as the public face of the split between the father of autonomy and the mother of dependency, with the separation intensifying under the inevitable weight of rationality from the public sphere. Rationality is all that saves men from their fear of being swallowed by the maternal. It also, inevitably, leads to the destruction of maternal values. It is depersonalised, abstract and calculable and neatly replaces any interaction involving personal relationships and traditional authority and belief. Benjamin points out that it makes a wonderful partner for bureaucratic systems – just like advanced capitalism! The denial of dependency is crucial for the bourgeois idea of individual freedom, which carries with it the illusion of choice so central to the perpetuation of the multiple myths of capitalism. The many Christs of erotic connection and empowerment stand as fundamental challenges to this foundational lie, proclaiming time and again that it is in us and through us that the world is transformed.

Benjamin offers a wonderful insight for me into how the size game works in our present world. It certainly cuts women off from owning their desires but it also sets up a reality of delusional autonomy that has to be preserved on many levels. In the Slim for Him and Weigh Down Diet programmes we saw how the false notions of democracy were held in place through the idea that one had total control over the size of one's body – it enabled other more political factors to be overlooked. In illustrating where patriarchy may be rooted Benjamin also alerts me to the great anxiety that it is necessary to instil in women over size. Men who have dealt with their own fears of the devouring maternal may be able to allow women to be whatever size they wish, and this in turn may mean that the edges of our world, economic and social, could be a little softer, less controlled and more relational. There is a lot at stake in this size question, all the edifices of the unequal world of the patriarchs that we inhabit. Once again we see the truth of Douglas's claims that the bodies of women are used to define the edges of male society.

Women's desire, is as we have seen, removed from us at a young age in the service of patriarchy and this removal does not go unmarked by us: we mark it with our bodies. It is here, in our bodies, then that I would argue we need to start if we are to overcome it. The claim that I am making is that women reclaiming their own desire will not generate a hierarchal system learnt through the skin; in short, women taking the right to the will for sex and power expressed through the size they wish to be will be a rebellion against not simply the body fascism of patriarchy but also many other aspects of that pernicious system. Women need to transform the need to be desired into an acceptance of desiring. This is, as we have seen, very difficult because we are trapped into other ways of being at a very early age and so live in the world of images rather than the world of embodied desire. To realise this may be one step in the right direction, but the journey is a long one because patriarchal society has cast so many negative images about female power that expressing any will to power is far from easy. Female needs, as we see from the work of Dinnerstein, Trask and Benjamin, are dangerous because they turn the order of things on its head. If women took what they wanted instead of attending to the needs of others patriarchy would be faced with a real problem. In order to deal with the issue of female power society either places it within a frame of dread and fear – the rampaging castrating female is a deep psychological truth if one is male – or makes it exotic – the dominatrix is not an object of fear but rather of satisfaction. Either way the real desires of real women are once again overlooked and sidelined.

As we have seen, it is the frustration of this desire for power and sex that is at the core of many eating disorders. And as long as we are objects to others as a result of being objects to ourselves with the disassociation that involves, we will always have eating disorders.

Women, desiring to be desired – go shopping!

Young-Eisendrath believes women give in to the anorexic beauty image precisely because their will for power does not simply go away, but moulds itself to what is possible within society. Male dominance and the psychology we have just examined mean that men have the power to dictate the body size they prefer, or more accurately can cope with in terms of their own psychological weakness. Woman then can aspire to share the dignity of man if she can become his object, but she can never share his power because she has nothing to give in this way that the world would receive.[30] In order to achieve the status of object of desire many women in this world take heed of the media bombardment of their psyches and begin to reshape their bodies. It is the case that very few people are grossly overweight and, as we have seen, the medical evidence which links all kinds of dire consequences with weight is questionable, but nevertheless women submit to the diet culture. Gradually the ideal woman emerges, but the ideal has to be maintained through an eating disorder because the female body is not meant to be devoid of fat and angular. Two rather contradictory things then happen for women: they have transformed themselves into objects of desire and at the same time they believe they have control. The realities of the world demonstrate that they do not actually have power, so the sense of control does not lead, as might have been hoped, to the fulfilment of one basic need – rather it leads to shame, guilt, self-consciousness and a need to be reassured that the image is still in place,[31] in other words a reality far from the self-confident and empowered women we wish to be. The reassurance is sought from the experts who tell us what to eat and when, and of course make a large amount of money in the process.

Young-Eisendrath believes that in order to step outside this object status and really find the power we need we have to face the hag in ourselves, that is, the overpowering female whose needs and desires are monstrous.[32] Being beautiful under patriarchy is not about our own power and desire, it is about power between men, and this is the system Young- Eisendrath urges us to move away from. Being the kind of beautiful that the male psyche can cope with takes a great deal of work and actually moves us away from our capacity for passion. She sees clearly how this works in the sexual arena: it actually makes women desire sex less because it is not an equal exchange of desires but rather a passive female being on the receiving end of the interests of another. There is little pleasure in this for women but they can substitute the seduction of power for sexual satisfaction. When the beautiful woman turns into the homely wife she is paid lip service as an honoured figure but Young-Eisendrath believes this is only because in this capacity she continues to serve the needs of others.[33] So once again even when women quite naturally get beyond the 'beauty trap' they are also served up to society as the nurturer of the needs of others, which perpetuates the denial of their own needs. Middle-aged spread then takes on a whole new cultural/psychological connotation!

Young-Eisendrath tells us that research shows that for women who are denied connection with their desire, shopping has a crucial role. In a world where men are the subjects and women the objects in a power game played on the skin, women do not simply give up a will to power or subjectivity – they just have to gain it through diverse means. Women shoppers are seduced into an atmosphere that promises them power of choice, promises that they can be subjects of their own desires. It is a means of escape from the resentment of having given personal control to others but still it does not wholly overcome the dilemma that women are in. That is to say, while exerting subjectivity through consumer object choice women are often buying those things which make them more desirable as objects of the male gaze.[34] Retailers seduce us into buying freedom when it is not really available and even if it were we live in a throwaway society. In order to be fully human we need to understand our desires and we have to face them, acceptable or not, because only when we know can we really choose to live an intentional life, one that is reclaimed from patriarchy, one that recovers the erotic unmoulded woman within each woman. This deep knowing depends on dialogue in community, and we as women are given manipulative dialogical partners who are patriarchal in one form or another. It becomes difficult to find our authentic desire under those circumstances and this frustration is carried on our bodily frames.

The erotic Christ and female desire

Liberation theology has to address this blocking of desire and will in women, and feminist theologies have begun to reframe Christologies that are erotic in nature. This erotic Christ does not restrict and deny bodily feelings but rather embraces and expands them. Within this understanding the starting point is to see God's creative power as the power to love and to be loved; this may seem no real move for women, who are, we have seen, encouraged to give themselves away in love. However, when we begin to realise that this is in fact not a self-sacrificial love at all but rather a grasping and living out of one's full potential in a relational, mutual exchange, then the picture changes considerably. Feminist theologians such as Carter Heyward[35] and myself[36] have claimed that God needed incarnation and that incarnation changes everything in terms of power relations. There is no longer a God above and beyond who dictates his will but rather a loving companion in the struggle who needs mutuality and relationality.

Heyward reimages divinity[37] as something we grow towards by choice and activity, drawn as we are by the power of the erotic that is our birthright. This lies in us as the power of dunamis, a biblical concept that Heyward claims Jesus wished to share. This implies the crucial ability to make choices, which has been limited for women and which as we have seen has an effect on their embodied living, literally on the size they manifest in the world. Restoring choice as part of the christological process rather than passive victimhood is contributing to a greater understanding of who God may be and who women are in relation to that God. Daly told us a long time ago that if god is male then the male is God and we have seen how this works in the lives of women who in infancy are expected to give up their power while men and boys may claim theirs. This re-imaging by Heyward goes a long way to restoring the power balance, to enable women to take hold of the power that is their birthright too and express their passions through and within a divine process of becoming. This is a revolution – if the God women follow frees and empowers them in this way then the restricting discourses of patriarchy will be seen for what they are, blasphemous, because they do not acknowledge let alone encourage the full becoming of the divine incarnate in the bodies of women.

Erotic power is wild, uncontrolled and beautiful, all that the female body is not allowed to be under patriarchal control. Further, erotic power and embodied knowing involve subjective engagement of the whole self in relationship, and subjectivity has not been encouraged in women. This shift in christological thinking requires that authority and power are viewed differently. Heyward is anxious to move away from the idea that authority is something that is exercised over us by God or state, and to come to an understanding of it as possessed by the self. Heyward notes that two words are used in the gospels. One is *exousia* which denotes power that has been granted, whereas *dunamis* which is raw power, innate, spontaneous and often fearful, is not granted – it is inborn, and this is the authority that Jesus claims. What was new about Jesus was his realisation that our dunamis is rooted in God and is the force by which we claim our divinity. By acting with dunamis we, just like Jesus, act from both our human and divine elements. The suspicion of human power and initiative that is deeply rooted in our religious understanding can be overcome by the story of Eve and her actions in Eden, a story that is in fact incredibly good news for women, especially in relation to the issues of food and eating. In addition when we acknowledge dunamis and not exousia, our relation with the divine and others becomes an erotic dance of empowerment and not a crippling and disempowering struggle for self-control and contained bodies. There are real possibilities, then, in this new christological understanding for empowering women, placing before them as the model woman an erotically engaged, relational yet autonomous human/divine mature person, fully embodied. This is a model of Christian womanhood that we have not seen in the recent Jesus diet programmes or indeed throughout the history of Christianity.

For Heyward intimacy is the deepest quality of relation, and she sees no reason why it should be left out of our theological story, indeed she does not see such a thing as possible. Heyward believes that to be intimate is to be assured that we are known in such a way that the mutuality of our relation is real, creative and co-operative, and so it has a fundamental part in any theology and religious practice. While Heyward argues that part of the message of Jesus was that we too have this power which can be found through intimate relation she also says we see that people are afraid of this power. She writes: 'The crucifixion signals the extent to which human beings will go to avoid our own relational possibilities.'[38] This fear may have been set in place as a male psychic reality stemming from fear of being swallowed by the mother, so it is not a human condition at all, just a condition of one half of the human race – but a condition that cripples the other half. An erotic Christology is fully embodied, sensuous and seeking vulnerable commitment, alive with expectancy and power. This Christ enables women to find their subjectivity and power, in other words to live more fully in their skins. It seems to me that this sensuous knowing is an essential part of a Fat Jesus and, as we have seen, there is a gospel argument for it!

Healthy anorexia?

It would not be fair to leave this chapter without examining a rather different argument. Catherine Garrett,[39] like many other specialists in the area of eating disorders, is clear that they are not pathologies or diseases but rather entirely social phenomena, so that the anorexic body for her is a text to be deciphered. This book has taken such an approach as read, but Garrett takes an interesting turn with this approach since she believes that spiritual pain is a very positive part of the condition and is not a problem to be solved but a question to be lived. The liberation theologian in me rebels – after all, watching pain and allowing it to continue if one has any power at all to stop it is one theological premise that feminist theologians have been working long and hard to overcome. Garrett's starting point is that anorexia involves many ritualistic patterns that in themselves may be useful and allow a reconnection with the world in a totally different fashion, once one has lived the journey. Her book is based on the stories of those who have recovered or are recovering from anorexia as well as the detailed accounts by those who have died. In this respect feminist theology has to take seriously the experiential nature of the theory. Certainly she sees anorexia as a search for meaning on the part of those who develop that way of life and she argues that many of those who recover cite a higher power external to themselves as crucial to their recovery. This is very interesting since many who actually develop anorexia also speak of a higher power, often as a male voice that tells them not to eat.

Having considered thousands of accounts by anorexics, Garrett says she feels compelled to wonder whether anorexia is a precursor to recovery or a journey in itself. If medieval women fasters were seen as saints, then how are we to view modern day anorexics? Garrett is not asking if we can see the medieval women as anorexic – her question is a little more subtle than that: if asceticism has any meaning, how do we translate it in relation to anorexics? She says that anorexics are usually assumed to be under the influence of purely secular society, but she argues that many anorexics are fasting for religious reasons and from spiritual motivation. We have seen this in the lives of many contemporary Christian women, the most famous perhaps being Simone Weil. Jo Ind, author of *Fat is a Spiritual Issue*,[40] could also be seen as a religious anorexic of the modern world. In her account she tells us that she took Jesus fasting in the wilderness as an example and so would see food as a sin and pray that she might be released from her desire for it.[41] She was never overweight, but she did love food and this for her was the sin, loving something more than you loved God. It meant that she had to control that love, but of course that control also meant that she lost touch with her body and what it wanted. There was no help for her because, as she tells us, her church was not very good with bodies. Many of the stories that Garrett relays have what we may call negative spiritual motivation, while some others have a far more positive spiritual motivation: some women understand their asceticism as in some way atoning for the world. It seems, then, that despite the relentless medicalisation and secularisation of anorexia there still remains a spiritual element for some of the women who take this path. Garrett points out that because most women who are anorexic are at the mercy of the secular system, they are let down by its failure 'to provide rituals of re-incorporation after a period of liminal asceticism'.[42] In other words, women who quite legitimately, in Garrett's view, take the path of fasting to the point of starvation are not aided and indeed may be made worse by a system that has no room in it for the spiritual practice of extreme asceticism. She argues that many of these people who in a sane and free way enter an ascetic path may become mentally ill because of the way in which they are forced to accomplish their transition alone using private symbols.[43] Garrett is arguing for the spiritual power of extreme asceticism to be recognised in the medical profession, but we also have to say that it would need to be recognised again in most religious traditions, which have for some time questioned it and tamed it. She wants a more radical approach that addresses the existential and spiritual questions inherent in an anorexic way of life and she also wants the rituals that can aid a transition. Garrett recounts many cases where the women felt the need to reconnect, and they used sex as the way to do it. Through these encounters they felt better about themselves and learnt once again how to live in the body in the presence of another. From the point of view of the erotic Christ, the fully embodied and passionate one, this is an interesting road to reintegration since it is skin on skin as a witness to the fullness of one's humanity. Certainly a return to the body as Trask suggests along with the many rituals of embodiment that are available to us as well as the rituals of communal eating that are central to the Christian life may be amongst the array of things offered to those who have taken an ascetic path and are being welcomed back as honoured friend. Of course as a feminist liberation theologian I would hope that women do not have to treat their bodies in such extreme ways to find spiritual meaning. However, as we have seen, women do, so Garrett's call for rituals of integration may be well heeded by the community.

I hope this chapter has shown how women's inability to claim their desire is at the heart of many eating disorders and that through an examination of this we have seen some ways through it. What was once seen as a universal absolute can now be traced to a psychological weakness on the part of the male psyche and women can begin to see what is needed for their own healing and empowerment. There are many parts to this reclaiming of desire, from language to patterns of nurture, and the ways in which we relate in our most intimate moments. Power, sex and size are all related matters for women, and the erotic Christ as part of an emerging Fat Jesus is one step on the way to integrating all these aspects in an empowered incarnational rebellion. What we come to realise is that the crippling reality of patriarchy actually sits on very few pillars; it would be foolish to think these are not well bedded in but also defeatist to believe they cannot come tumbling down. The power to make this happen does lie in the bodies of women but these bodies have to find their subjectivity. We must declare our beauty, our power and our desires and realise that 'a woman's authentic beauty first comes into existence when her body expresses her self acceptance – the harmony or the condition of the fully conscious creative struggle she has achieved within herself.'[44] There is no doubt that the legacy of a disembodied, dualistic God has not served women well and it is the task of contemporary theology to address that painful issue.

When within the Christian tradition will we be able to say along with a woman whom Chernin interviewed, 'I'm in a glory of fleshy existence, I see power in it, in my own body, fertility and abundance. A large unrestricted sense of life.[45] I dream about huge women.'[46] Perhaps when we have a Fat Jesus!

Chapter Five

Breaking bread with ourselves

'Happy are those who hunger and thirst for what is right:
they shall be satisfied.' (Matthew 5:6)

Fat is the 'screw you' to prescribed social roles.[1]

As we have come to see, body size has increasingly taken a role in the production of female identity, worth and subjectivity over the last century. Slenderness has come to signify beauty, which in turn has created a hierarchy based on physical difference which has led into the supposed fulfilment of material privilege. On the other side of the equation we have the fat body which has increasingly been viewed with suspicion and even disgust as a deeply morally flawed form of embodiment, chaos-driven and lacking control. As we have seen, fat phobia also holds in place many social structures and the fat bodies of women have under certain circumstances come to carry economic and racial overtones. In the West most young girls know what dieting is and many have already tried it by a very young age even when they had no need. This is in stark contrast with, for example, Kenyan women who when surveyed did not understand the concept of dieting and (as mentioned earlier) Samoan women who glory in their abundant flesh. What we eat and what we do not eat appears to create a much larger scale of values than can be carried in the food itself. Lelwica has argued that secular explanations of food and dieting, medical and aesthetic, can not fully convey what is at stake here because they lack the subtlety to delve into the many layers of symbolism with which both these things have been invested.

Beginning from the purely medical, when considering size means that we lose sight of 'its capacity to suggest a picture of the ideal social and cosmic order and to unify experience within that grand scheme'.[2] We have to acknowledge that women's bodies carry a great deal of societal significance and so dieting has become a cultural rite of womanhood in which her 'fears and dreams are generated and regulated and the prevailing social order negotiated and reproduced'.[3] In the absence of rites of passage for young girls we have offered them a diet culture in which we will remove from them their physical desires, their sense of self-worth and their empowerment, in short we will remove them from the stuff of life, their birthright, their dunamis. We will send them away from home – the home of their divine/human becoming, their bodies.

Sugar, pills and shopping

In so doing we also deliver them into the hands of the markets which have been quick to capitalise on the anxiety we create in women. At their most insidious these markets have been created by the pharmaceutical companies who offer salvation to the grossly overweight through magic pills and potions. Of course these miracles come at a physical price – they are filled with phenyl-propanolamine which is linked with kidney failure, heart disease, hypertension and strokes. Despite this over five million women have been put on them. Other diet pills contain fenfluramine and selective serotonin reuptake inhibitors which damage neurons and result in sleep disorders and mood swings. Yet these too are prescribed and the restrictions on them are far less than those imposed on the surgical options women are advised to consider such as stomach stapling and biliopancreatic division. These are still offered in cases of so-called morbid obesity where there are often some health problems. The death rate from this surgery is high, but that is not mentioned. Both these options will be successful in a society driven by scorn for the fat body and no one will regulate the harm done by the pharmaceutical companies because in a way the fat deserve what they get. Even sociologists who have understood the power and politics in the construction of the anorexic body have paid very little attention to the fat body and the construction of its politics. Perhaps it is the Marxist in me but when I see profits such as £33 billion annually on the diet industry, with the Jesus diet industries having a fair slice (£20 billion annually on cosmetics and £300 million annually on surgery), I see politics. The economy of the West would suffer if women opted out of the expected norm and this could never be allowed. As Lelwica tells us, 'The profit-seeking ethos of consumer capitalism seems both omnipresent and omniscient supplanting an omnipotent creator as the invisible source of transcendent power. Given its quasi-religious function it is not surprising that some of this system's rhetorical manoeuvres selectively employ certain terms and conventions of traditional religion.'[4] She notes that personal confessions are usual in advertisements for diet products and diet rituals are framed as a search for meaning. The Lite products are meant to give the impression of enlightenment and they are advertised as saving marriages and bringing greater happiness to those who consume them. The saving words on these products are 'low-cal' and 'fat free'. Of course this is misleading because, as Slim Fast knows only too well, if you want people to keep coming back then you have to put something in that is appealing. This something is sugar, masses of it, and it made Slim Fast profits of £520 million last year. The real health risks of this are great as we know, compared to the imagined risks that the majority of women who use their products actually face. Dieting is a wonderful invention for capitalism, as paradoxical as that may sound – as most dieters never succeed in keeping weight off because many should not have dieted in the first place and their weight gain is simply the body returning to where it should naturally be, so that the industry has a stream of endless dieters. In addition dieting makes people consume more, if not food then other products as a compensation for their lack of food satisfaction. As we saw in the last chapter, women shop to help them feel in control in a world that does not naturally and willingly give them that control. There is nothing like a diet to make women feel out of control and so in need of some soothing shopping to restore the imaginary balance.

Lelwica is not the first to suggest that the rather narrow promise of salvation offered by the diet-product manufacturers acts as a distracting mechanism from the real problems in the world; as she puts it, Culture Lite 'gives you the right to change your thighs, not the world'.[5] It is, then, a central player in society's politics of distraction, which gives me much to think about in relation to the ever growing evangelical diet programmes which have combined the obsession with thinness, fundamentalist piety and big business in a very effective way. Christianity, it seems, is being easily integrated into the culture of consumerism and profit, and for a liberation theologian this is an alarming turn of events. Could it be argued that a Christian community that has moved furthest from the primitive eating communities that were certainly at the heart of Christian eucharistic thinking has become so individualist that it actually promotes the notion of individual personal salvation through the right shape and size? This is, I am sure, a very controversial suggestion but one that is not without foundations. I believe, after all, the religion of the Word does prioritise the individual response whereas a sacramental eating community appears to have a less self-orientated notion of salvation. We saw that even with the fasting saints there was a social dimension that appears to be entirely absent in the Slim for Him programmes and the Weigh Down Diet: in the latter, ordering, and not eating, vast quantities of food is seen as faith in the power of God to provide, a blessing from God rather than a sin against humanity. The all-important thing is to realise that the devil tempts with food and so control and resistance are the keys to the kingdom.

This religious flavour in the world of dieting is not only found in the religious right's approach, it is there in almost all the secular diet groups in the West. We have seen that this may be because of the dualism inherited from Christianity that still remains within our culture despite its insistence that it is fully secular. Many diet programmes tell us we are allowed so many sins a day while others offer us the 'born again' treatment: all our sins will be washed away with each pound we shed and life will be seen anew, new chances, old ways overcome. This really is that old-time religion, except that it is not, which is what I find so worrying. It is my view that when people forget the roots of the oppressive systems that they place themselves in, such as diet groups, then they also forfeit the tools to deal with those choking roots. In other words the kind of body-controlling and denying dualism that is at the heart of much secular understanding of size and the body cannot be confronted and overcome simply because the roots are not understood. In my view a grasp of incarnational theology as it could be expressed is one very effective tool in the battle against the destructive split of patriarchal thinking. Blind as secular culture is to its deeply embedded Christian roots, it is also devoid of the equipment to look again at what simply seems to be a natural and healthy way of life.

Converting to slenderness

Kandi Stinson[6] has carried out interesting research that high-lights the ways in which the secular weight-loss programmes still have a religious feel to them and as such also tap into surprising depths within the psyches of the women who attend them. It is astonishing to learn that 65 million people at any one time are on weight loss programmes in the United Sates and that more money is spent on them than on social services and education.[7] A classic example, then, of reducing one's thighs and not attending to the world.

Stinson alerts us to the fact that even the motivations for attending a weight-loss programme have some religious ele-ments to them such as a desire to grow as a person – one would wonder how this could be achieved unless there is an ingrained assumption that being overweight is being a denuded person. Interestingly the Protestant work ethic is to be seen here too in a couple of ways: first, those who participate see the programmes as work and they measure their success or failure in the same lan-guage as they would apply to their working lives – a disciplined approach leads to high-yield outcomes, weight loss, while lazi-ness has no outcomes. These outcomes within the capitalist system that grew from the Protestant work ethic[8] need to be pre-dictable and calculable which of course weight loss is under these rather superficial programmes. In addition the self-help literature of these groups also talks about people as if they were products that can be endlessly changed and improved with hard work and the right tools.[9] Within this scheme, joining a group is similar to an act of conversion, especially as part of what then happens is a public act of confession regarding weakness around food and a renewed act of faith that one will overcome and find strength again. Stinson believes these are less than useful 'religious' communities because while using much of the language they actually play up guilt and surveillance while playing down community, emotion and ritual.[10] In this way they are tapping into deep memories but not being prepared to go the whole way with the community that the Christian Church is meant to provide. They are also very damaging to women's self-esteem: we have seen elsewhere how women are susceptible to guilt and low self-worth, which of course the confessions of not having enough control and failure would encourage, but we have also seen that women find ritual and emotion very important for their full becoming. These secular programmes, then, appear to be using the worst of religion and not actually delivering the salvation they promise.

Stinson, who is making her research in the context of the United States, demonstrates how religion in that context has bent under the weight of capitalism, becoming more individualistic with mega churches offering small groups, coffee shops and exercise classes. Along with these fairly innocuous groups there are also self-help classes attached to the new mega churches and the religious language, once the domain of theology and religion alone, has leaked into these groups. The crossover has not been as productive as people may imagine because what has emerged is a literature that makes the individual the problem and takes away any political importance that there may be. The analysis of any problem then becomes very shallow and individually focused and, as Stinson points out, the causes remain untouched.[11] She uses the example of addiction to illustrate the point: if addiction becomes individualised then it becomes a point for despair and feelings of lack of control. The insatiability inherent in addiction is never analysed in a wider cultural context and of course it is not in the interests of capitalism for it to be – insatiability is after all the very heart of a consumerist capitalist system. However, if we were to understand this insatiability in a more political context we might find that the worst excesses of capitalism were combated. Why is it that we feel so empty and so vulnerable? As we saw earlier, Rita Brock believes it is because we are 'born so open to the presence of others in the world it gives us the enormous, creative capacity to make life whole. Yet such openness means that the terrifying and destructive factors of life are also taken into the self, a self that then requires loving presence to be restored to grace.'[12] In the consumer-driven individualistic world in which we live we rarely find the loving presence we need to be restored. Brock urges us to find our heart and realise how we have been damaged and our original grace distorted. This is not in order that we may dwell in victimhood but rather that we may be able to understand the community aspect of our lives as well as connect with the anger necessary for action that comes when we see how the systems under which we live act to keep us broken-hearted.

Brock, like Heyward, believes that it is connection with our deepest passions that awakens us to our erotic power; a power that is enhanced by relationship, not by control and dominance. A power, then, that places us against the control of right-wing religion and capitalism and urges us into a passionate embrace of our deepest feelings and longings. Erotic power and embodied knowing involve subjective engagement of the whole self in relationship.[13] Brock claims that divine reality and redemption are love in all its fullness, an embodied love beating in the heart of a broken-hearted healer. Crucially this model also gives autonomy to women as we realise that our brokenness under the tyranny of gender is the strength of the broken-hearted healer, the way in fact to begin to look again at the grief of humanity, as Dinnerstein would say – the way, therefore, within the present context, to enable women to overcome the destructive patterns put in place so early in life, to enable a sense of self-worth and to satisfy the insatiable cravings that make us so open to manipulation by the markets. Brock's understanding of Christology propels us away from the shallow analysis of the self-help literature and into a political engagement with the many material causes of our broken-heartedness. This may be our strength but it also calls us to address the issues that hurt us.

Stinson describes how in the groups she studied there was a very strong concept of temptation being everywhere to do with food, and the language of falling from grace was common. The struggle of good and evil was an equally prevalent theme even with videos being shown that demonstrated internal struggles between the good self and the bad self. Within this scheme not eating was seen as a way of truly valuing yourself and so taking care of oneself became equated with self-deprivation.[14] This is a nasty twist on the feminist call for women to put their needs first, as these groups do claim that they are offering feminist options for women to take care of themselves but, as we have seen, the kind of care is dubious. The apolitical nature of this care we are meant to take can be seen in one particular video that Stinson mentions in which a woman arrives home from work after a long day and then receives a phone call from work. In the course of a very long conversation she eats almost a whole cake, and then feels guilty. The narrative revolves around the food and the woman's lack of control; it is mentioned that she would be stressed by this event but nevertheless the 'blame' is placed at her door and no questions are asked about the exploitation by her employers in making their unreasonable demands with this after-hours home invasion. Of course we should not be too surprised by this since the kind of caretaking that these weight-loss groups promote is just the kind that will deliver us into the genocidal working patterns that capitalism loves and our bodies hate. After all, women in diet programmes have come to ignore what their bodies are really telling them and have replaced that affectionate conversation for a monologue of control, discipline and deprivation. This is classic Christian dualism and the split goes deeper in seeing thin as good and fat as evil. Punishment in these programmes comes in the form of exercise not purgatory, but it does allow people to eat the occasional thing that would otherwise be completely banned from their diets. This kind of delayed gratification is at the very heart of traditional Christian salvation narratives where the believer is told to endure here on earth and await the rewards in heaven. It is also at the very heart of advanced capitalism in which we work harder, get more in debt and are told and believe that it is all leading to a paradise of materialism in which we are blessed. Alice Miller amongst others has demonstrated just how damaging this arrangement is for the human psyche, as it splits us within ourselves and deadens our inner voice.

Stinson[15] points out that in religious cultures where there is fasting there is usually feasting as well and so the community aspect of food rituals is held in place. By contrast, the dieting culture and, at its most extreme, the anorexia culture do not have feasts and so the participants become very isolated within their own food restrictions. It is difficult for them to eat with friends in case they are tempted to sin and public eating is extremely dangerous as there is no control over what goes into the food. Lack of connection becomes a real issue for those who are in this world of dieting and this is quite the reverse of what an eating community should be, far removed from the Messianic Banquet and the company of vulnerable healers. The before-and-after stories of miserable lives transformed through the mill of dieting cultures are nothing less than stories of the salvation of grace, but of course they can never be complete since so many gain the weight they lost and have to restart the endless toil of deprivation and isolation. Of course the fundamental question of what weight has to do with who we really are is never addressed. Rather, images are peddled of who we should be and how happy it will make us. The body that is actually assumed to be present in reality disappears under the rhetoric and in this way all the talk of personal transformation is in fact rather disembodied. To this theologian that is not so unlike the traditional notions of salvation, where as women we simply had to disembody to sample the delights of heaven, we had to become half angel and half man. I would wish to argue that the firm, hard and slender body that is the ideal of these programmes equates to the man while the angel is that part that just floats above it all – the apolitical woman/child.

This situation of disembodiment in my view takes a rather sinister turn when Stinson tell us of Overeaters Anonymous which was founded in 1960. This organisation believes that control and willpower are never enough in our human bodies and what we have to do is find the willpower to give it all over to a higher power. The first three steps of the inevitable twelve-step plan encourage people to realise their helplessness, believe in a higher power who can restore sanity and turn one's life over to God.[16] This is a feminist nightmare in three steps! Such a programme is aimed at demoralising and disempowering, in my view, since it not only encourages a person to believe she is helpless but also that there is some mental illness involved in overeating. Once again the individual is targeted and self-worth

attacked. Stinson points out that what was missing in all the programmes she examined was the political issue of good and
affordable nutritious food. Why am I not surprised?

Snacking and the Last Supper

Snacking has become almost a pastime in most western cultures
and while there may be some nutritional advantage to taking
small amounts more often this is not how it has worked out. The
multinationals have seen an opportunity to provide more snack
foods, which they produce with high levels of sugar and fat, at
very low costs. In the 1960s they produced about 250 new
products a year; this leapt to 2,000 new products by the 1980s.[17]
There is, as one might expect, an economic dimension to this: the
poor appear to be the most avid snackers and their health is
affected accordingly. Perhaps the most worrying aspect of this
cheap and nasty food is that it is now franchising itself into
schools. Pizza Hut and Taco Bell offer many financial incentives
to schools to allow them to run the food franchises and the
schools are happy to be helped with decreasing budgets while the
children are happy because they eat that kind of food at home
anyway. However, the pizza that they would eat at home or
would previously have eaten in school cafeterias was half the size
than that which is now on offer with the new franchises. The new
size provides one-third of the daily calorific intake for school-age
children. Coca Cola also has a school franchise and it was
estimated that each child drank 40.3 gallons a year. North
Americans of all ages have access to cheap poor quality food, and
as such it is a country that pays little attention to the true
well-being of its people, who, I would like to argue, need the
sensuous delight of non-processed food to celebrate their
embodiment.

Of course there are environmental issues involved in all this
cheap food. One can of diet drink provides one calorie of food
energy, but 'costs 800 kilocalories in fuel, involves land destroy-
ing strip mining, pollutes the soil, water and groundwater with
toxic minerals and uses up more water than the soda in the can'.[18]
We all know of course that food travels further than it ever did to
get to our tables. so the environmental cost is larger than ever. In

addition the increased demand for meat is placing a huge strain on the planet and subsidies to richer countries mean that smaller farmers in less developed countries are being undercut; they then have to change their farming habits. Many poor countries have to export their crops to pay off debts and this means that they are left with less to feed their own people. In very real terms the multinationals decide who will eat and what they will eat, which makes a mockery of the naive idea that weight loss is a democratising activity. Indeed in terms of food distribution there is no will to design a system that would make food available to everyone, although this is entirely possible and all would have enough to eat, but rather the concern is to maximise the profits.[19] There appears to be no call either from the consumers for this more equitable distribution, which may be because eating has become a dissocialised and fragmented experience for most of us. It is something that we often do alone, and very rarely if we ever consider how the food got to our tables and at what cost.

This is light years away from the eating communities of the past and indeed from the eucharistic enactments inaugurated at the Last Supper. Monica Hellwig has argued that the way in which we view the 'hunger of the world' should always be within the context of the Last Supper which was, as she sees it, the foundational meal of Christianity. The context was one of oppression and the act of communal eating a commitment of ultimate fellowship, the kind that would be embodied through these continued acts of eating and radical praxis. I would like to suggest that what one ingested was the passion of Christ understood not as a final sacrifice but as a radical way of living countercultural praxis through the skin. We are fed with incarnation possibilities and sustained to ever widen the boundaries of this contained patriarchal order that does nothing to embrace and allow for the flourishing of our divine/human reality. Hunger, Hellwig tells us, is a powerful experience that drives us to action, that is, if it is not self-induced and prolonged when, as we have seen, it brings with it inertia.

Behold: the Fat Jesus

The Fat Jesus wants us to hunger and indeed shares that hunger with us, but this is not a desperate search for satisfaction – it is rather a continued commitment to expanding the edges through sharing and creative engagement with each other and the resources of the planet. It is a traditional theological understanding amongst those from a high sacramental strand of Christianity to see connections between the feeding of the five thousand and the Last Supper. The former is seen to be a precursor to the latter which is understood to be the ultimate food. I do not wish to spend time arguing the point; rather, I wish to see the connection lying in a radical commitment to feeding the world when we eat from that eucharistic table. As we have seen, there is enough for each person on the planet to have 2,500 calories a day, in short, enough that no one need die from lack of food. This commitment, then, is political rather than one that encourages us to starve ourselves, which does nothing. The Fat Jesus compels us to demand fairer production policies, better quality food, more equitable distribution and enough food on all tables, food that we eat with passion, with joy, with embodied pleasure, not praising God for his blessing and then binning it! The Fat Jesus does not wish us to control our desire for food but rather to passionately engage with a desire for the world to eat and to celebrate the life that is enhanced through this abundance. Some years ago the theologian Tissa Balasuriya[20] urged Catholics to suspend the celebration of the Eucharist until such time as all were equal at the table. His argument was that around that table we proclaim the inclusion and equality of all in a world that in reality is unequal and excluding; his solution was then a suspension as a political act akin to individual hunger strikes in order to bring to the attention of global governments the need for radical change. I understand his motivation and indeed can see a place for such an action, but looking at the question from the perspective of women does put another light on it. Women around the world, either through dieting cultures or because of the unequal distribution of food, are every day the ones who do not get enough, so that asking that they get less, even in symbolic terms, does not seem the most radical praxis. Indeed, it is the power of the symbolic nature of food in the lives of women and, by extension, in patriarchal society that has been the focus of this book; women have carried much patriarchal cultural and psychic baggage that has expressed itself in wanting less flesh on women's bones and demanding that women are less in society. Within this context celebratory eating is a revolutionary step in itself, but when we realise what this may mean for women who will also be reconnecting with their desires and sense of power through this passionate eating we begin to understand just how revolutionary this Fat Jesus is calling us to be.

We perhaps need to follow the example of Jesus of Nazareth and use food and drink in such a way that we too will be called gluttons! After all he was proclaiming the kingdom of God through his eating and drinking with many of the outcasts of his day. Here was a statement in itself about the nature of the world he asked us to commit to in sharing his table. However, I think this has other implications too which are fundamental to who we are. We fail to see that our appetites can be an asset since they reveal to us the centrality of desire in our full functioning as a human person; desire is one of the deepest principles of life.[21] As we have seen, Heyward and I believe desire is the heart of our divine/human reality because it most fully connects us with ourselves and also propels us outward into relationality, mutuality and vulnerability. It is something to be embraced and there has been a false and damaging distinction between one's desire for God and one's desire for the 'things of the world'. This desire is rooted in our dunamis, our erotic/divine natures, and as such needs to be acknowledged and celebrated in a Christian life. It is this attempt to control passion within Christian theology and religious practice that has actually badly backfired, cutting us off from our deepest passions in order that we become disconnected from each other. This has meant in the area of sexuality, for example, that the behaviours that the churches meant to stop through a warning against passion have simply increased and become even more meaningless, because we are not rooted in who we are. It is as though we are in a dream and simply inhabiting our bodies rather than fully living in them. Of course, when we are thus disconnected we are also at the mercy of the manipulation of the markets since we are adrift from our 'guts' (which is where the gospels tell us the true Christian life happens: *metanoia*, the word for conversion, means a turning over of one's guts) and constantly in need of something to supply meaning. As we have seen, the markets are only too willing to supply any range of meaning that will leave us craving more, whether this is because of the addictive additions to food or simply because of the superficiality of the meaning supplied.

Shannon Jung reminds us that eating and food have always been an expression of humans' relationship with God, and he also argues that they are an expression of our deepest values. He claims 'eating is a spiritual practice that reminds us who we are'[22] not only in our own bodies but also in relation to the world economy. Jung believes that we have forgotten the purpose behind the blessing of food and have been satisfied with an impoverished appreciation of eating. Once again we see how the Christian distrust of desires and appetites has led to a disconnection from an essential human/divine activity. For Jung there are very embodied consequences that stem from this impoverishment: two world-views actually emerge – one that is holistic and revolves around relationships and sharing while the other is business-orientated and involves slicing life up into bits.[23] He argues that eating is an intimate act which signifies how the world enters into us and how we become part of it; food can then be a source of grace and revelation or it can be simply fodder for management and control. In this way, then, food and eating are performative acts displaying the Christian life. We are familiar with Judith Butler's notion of performativity of gender whereby things that have no substance and reality in themselves are given life and meaning through their repeated performance. Christians too can give meaning through their repeated joyous embrace of what we may call 'dunamis eating', that is, their connection with the raw and passionate heart of their divine/human natures which will propel them into greater connection and relationality in the world. This manner of engaging with food and eating might counter what I have earlier suggested is an alarming manifestation of 'secular metaphysics'. This is a not entirely unexpected phenomenon in a secular world that has attempted so completely to erase the religious that it has forgotten what its heritage is. It has meant that the damaging split of body and spirit so beloved by the Church Fathers has continued in our society as the erroneous belief that mind and body are not one and that mind can control the unruly passions of the body.

For an incarnational theologian this continuation signals the degree to which we continue to believe that the heavens have not been collapsed by incarnation, a residue remains of unresolved metaphysics. We are still not at home in our flesh and so we fail to live the radical co-creative and co-redemptive implications of that reality. We will not fully commit to flesh and so we live as though we inhabited somewhere else. Of course the Christian understanding of incarnation shows us to what extent that living somewhere else did not work for God either, he too had to finally commit to the risk and vulnerability of flesh. We are told that God abandoned himself to flesh but we, who claim to follow, will never do the same – we always attempt to control it through various discourses of gender, race, class and size. The truly world-transforming power of incarnation will always be delayed as long as we continue to live as though Greek metaphysics had won the day rather than the full enfleshment of the fully human/divine God. There are of course cracks in this dualistic dialogue within the secular world as there always have been in the theological and religious worlds, but there is no serious attempt to incorporate the radical implications of a counter-understanding since the markets and advanced capitalism benefit from the rupture in the human condition just as the Church coffers did in days gone by. A marvellous counter to this way of thinking would be the Fat Jesus – the one with the flexible edges, edges that are not constantly policed by the guardians of improved selves and manicured lives. Signalling that vulnerability and not control, softness and not self-censure are central to a Christian life may throw light on the worst excesses of secular culture. As followers of Jesus we are 'sensuous revolutionaries' living our deepest passions and connections in order that our free and full embodiment may sing of abundant incarnation. The Fat Jesus who calls to us is in a true sense himself a sensuous hedonist empowering revolution through the skin and enabling abundant embodied living that is the counter to the worst excesses of our genocidal and disconnected world.

We have seen how Orbach and others agree with Jung that

bodies affect the environments they are in, and therefore how the female body entering what had previously been the male terrain of business had to become harder, more muscular and angular in order to not pose a threat to the system itself, rather than simply the men within it. The systems that have been built on separation, independence and control cannot have within them any hint of the maternal because the fear of the alternative values this holds would be overwhelming. The fear that the patriarchal order would crumble in the face of the devouring maternal is a real fear for those patriarchs who have built empires through living their lives running from the intimacy with the mother from whom they felt removed, a separation from which they have never recovered. Fat women, therefore, have to be removed from corporate life as they literally embody a set of conflicting values that threaten. There is not only room but an extreme need for the presence of the Fat Jesus and her sisters in the public world of the patriarchs; they need to carry their threat and their alternative life proudly on their broad shoulders and rolling Amazon hips.

Jung argues that in losing the spiritual significance of food we also lose its ecological significance because we reduce it to a function[24] rather than an organic presence. It comes to our tables with an ecological history and through human labour but both are lost in this world that never fully connects with it. We have seen how there have been connections between the disrespect for women's bodies and that for the body of the earth, and in the same way we can say that there is also disrespect for women's labour as well as that of the earth herself. The arguments for the reasons the Christian tradition lends itself to such a state of affairs do not need to be rehearsed, but we do well to acknowledge that this tradition has not served the earth and its inhabitants well in this matter.

If we are to believe feminist anthropologists – and I do accept that the jury is out – then there was a time when this ecologically friendly, non-competitive and peaceful relational society existed. It was the time when the divine was imaged as female but not simply female, rather as a large, fleshy mound of divinity. Amongst the earliest known depictions of the divine was the Venus of Willendorf, who has mountainous breasts and a vast belly, her hips move round to a huge ass, she is 'a sweeping hill of flesh'.[25] Most of these statues show the genitals of these women as huge and genuinely erotic rather than pornographic. Were they fashioned in cultures where men could face the site of their birth with no fear to their maleness, and what part did women play in enabling this? Of course like other fat women since their time they have suffered at the hands of male anthropologists, who have considered they had to be pregnant fertility figures because they could not simply be fat goddesses. Here we see the impossibility of divine subjectivity in fat form par excellence, even projected back in history. Certainly some of these figures were fertility goddesses used in rituals but these 'lovely ladies abounding in the lush landscapes that compose their visions of paradise'[26] also had other functions. The Venus of Laussel has rolls of flesh, curvaceous hips and pendulous breasts; her delicate fingers sit on her mountainous belly and her head is turned to suck on what she has in one hand. This is a powerful symbol for women – is it a phallus she has in her hand or is it the horn of plenty? Can it be transformed from one to the other through women touching their own flesh in the way she touches hers as a sign of the mysterious, powerful beauty that lies within? This divine woman is enfleshed and she rejoices in the horn of plenty – how did we get from here to the skinny Christ, the one who looks emaciated and drawn? What we can see is that with the restriction of the divine female body and its connection to the earth came a restriction of the female body that in turn has led to, or perhaps gone hand in hand with, a philosophy of control of the earth. It seems imperative that both rebel against the controlling will of patriarchy. Thealogy has shown us how important an eco-approach is in our religious scheme but it too has been less then vigilant when it comes to matters of shape and size. Perhaps the Fat Jesus can unite ecotheology once again with the ample goddesses who loved their bodies and the earth. This time they will be incarnate in the full bodies of the women of the earth.

Of course we may be able to argue that these memories from prehistory, or even from the birth of each individual, if we wish to take a psychological approach, have left us always imaging utopia as abundant. Fat has always been the shape of utopia because no one dreams of living in a skinny land.[27] As we have seen, these memories are also present in Christian symbolism with images of the Messianic Banquet, the feast that signals the fullness of God's work, which I suggest as Christians we can see as the full enfleshment of incarnation in radical and inclusive living. Not all Christians hold this view. For many today, whose edges are controlled by the Slim for Him programmes and the Weigh Down Diet, this table of fulfilment can never be indulged in – looked at and appreciated but never ingested. It has been argued that when martyrdom in its brutal reality was no longer part of Christian history there were many within its ranks who understood the overcoming of the flesh to be continued through savage asceticism. If the outside world would no longer martyr them as a test of their faith then they would martyr themselves through self-denial and brutal treatment of their own bodies. In this way they believed they were casting out the devil and seeking paradise. In Chapter 2 we saw how this worked out in the lives of women from the medieval period and how the severe theology of self-harm and purging also incorporated a social dimension that was largely absent in the early days. With the Slim for Him and Weigh Down Diet industry we seem to be witnessing a very troubling manifestation of what I think can be called 'designer martyrdom', because there is no social awareness in these programmes at all and the God they claim to worship is indeed imagined to wear designer clothes. The aspirations of those who join the programmes are, as we saw, 'designer' in nature – their bodies have to be shaped in order to be clothes pegs for the blessings of God which come in Gucci bags. This designer martyrdom is a very narrow form of Christianity, which literally ends at the edges of one's own shaped, pummelled, pampered and moisturised skin. It takes a great deal of money and a great deal of time to be martyred in this way. It is of course also a manifestation of one of the great ironies – that the skinny bodies of the saved contrast starkly with the bodies of those who literally slave to make the designer clothes. The slender bodies of the women in the Third World who are paid very poorly are not the glorious designer bodies of salvation; they are tired, abused and often diseased bodies of the unnoticed. The Fat Jesus needs to be the impetus for our rebellion against this clothes-peg Christianity and the narrow world it creates.

The Fat Jesus has another important function which is related to diet industries of all kinds. Katherine Hayle[28] is concerned with the discourse that is emerging of the post-human, within which the body becomes simply a fashion accessory in itself rather than, as she sees it, the ground of our being. Under this nightmare scenario the body in all its fleshy humanity is dissolved into the grand illusion of disembodiment. This is the designer world gone mad, the body itself no more than an accessory in a 'beautiful life'. We can see how we have got here, but how do we avoid further heightening of this nightmare, which we can perhaps see beginning with the notion of designer babies, and bodies constantly under the knife in search for the perfect life? It seems that it may only be a very small step from using the body to hang fashion accessories to beginning to view the body in that way itself. The riotous uncontrollability of the Fat Jesus seems like one way to guard against that truly frightening day.

I think what has become apparent during the course of this book is that the fat body is viewed with disgust by many. Of course it is equally feared, as we have seen through the work of some feminist theorists working in the area of gender development. This fear is because, as Kristeva would say, it functions as the abject in our society. That is to say, fat bodies 'take up the burden of representing the horrors of the body itself for the culture at large'.[29] They are the walking reminder of corporeality which the West with its Christian roots has always found difficult to cope with. This cultural process of abjection makes it impossible to speak in any meaningful way of a fat person since it does not allow for a self to exist in such a body. Many fat women will recognise this situation, finding it extremely difficult to be seen and heard in society. The way in which fat people are spoken to about their size also appears to assume that no one lives in that body. So perhaps putting a self in a fat body is the kind of act of heresy that a Fat Jesus would commit, because doing such a thing would require that society think again about the way in which the body is abjected from the self. The Fat Jesus would be a call to Christianity and to society to heal the split between body and mind.

Fat women in society are viewed as either being defective or aggressive when they move from the weight norm, but perhaps they are just unruly. However, we have to realise that this perception is only in relation to the patriarchal society that would wish them to be thin. Against this background fat women are threatening because they appear to claim the power and desire that society would deny women. The fat body, rather like the grotesque body before it, represents multiplicity, a bulging, open body in the process of becoming which is completely out of keeping with a bounded theology and a bounded society. What appears to be emerging, then, is an obscene Christ – one who challenges all the boundaries and opens up the whole divine process.

Marcella Althaus-Reid has spoken of an obscene Christ, by which she means that obscenity uncovers what needs to be made visible. For example, she says that the black and feminist Christs are obscene as they uncover both racism and sexism inherent in Christology. Speaking of the necessity for the uncovering of Christ Althaus-Reid says, 'Any uncovering of Christ needs to follow that pattern of obscenity as disruptive and illuminating at the same time, because Christ and his symbolic construction continue in our history, according to our own moment of historical consciousness.'[30] For us this consciousness had shifted and it is a matter of theological deceit and even falsehood if we continue to construct Christologies on the old knowledge; we too need to create an obscene Christ in matters of shape and size. Why? Because we have seen the worlds that are created by fat phobia, fear of the maternal and glorying in the anorexic; all these worlds are in themselves a crime against the incarnational glory of individuals but they also feed into larger systems of oppression that fuel the patriarchal world. The Fat Jesus is obscene and while the patriarchal order is in place must remain as such but she also asks us profound questions which we need to answer in our skin. Is incarnation about fixed categories or fluidity, embracing and developing within the historical moment, enlivening and expanding – or in a very concrete way remaining the same for ever? Have we confused the vibrant, urgent unfolding of the divine with fixed patterns of behaviour and, most importantly, with fixed body shapes? I think we need the abject Fat Jesus who bulges out over all the edges and carries her embodiment proudly and differently in the world. Fat is indeed, as Orbach says, a 'screw you' to the world of prescribed social roles and it seems to me that the Fat Jesus calls us all to obscenely declare 'screw you' to the myriad manifestations of patriarchal conformity that enslave us and narrow the glory of our abundant life and our liberative praxis. The 'screw you' that becomes manifest is the outpouring of over-the-edges, multiple countercultural redemptive incarnations carried with passion in the bodies of women living differently.

We have seen how women have been cast out from their bodies through a combination of systems and psychological quirks, and I hope that some of the consequences of that have become clear, from deaths through eating disorders to an inability to claim passion and power within the world. The eating communities that were once central to us as humans have been fragmented and women have not been invited as honoured guests to the tables that remain. As Nelle Morton told us, the journey is home but this is a journey back to our bodies, to a place of once again inhabiting this vacant flesh that holds within it the divine incarnate. We are asked to once again touch and revel in our passions and desires, to touch, taste and see it is good. This invitation is laid out before us at the eucharistic table, a table that has become sterile and bounded but that in its inception was the radical space of sensuous engagement and commitment. It was here that the exchange model of a patriarchal society was challenged and the sharing of bread and politics ensured that patriarchy would always be challenged through this radical sharing. It is here that we are invited to refuse the assimilation of norms and to instead find countercultural ways of radical praxis, of living 'as if', that is to say, as if the fullness of divine/human incarnation was enfleshed. It is through these repeated incarnational performances that the co-creation and co-redemption become lived realities. The Fat Jesus refuses the 'normal, the narrow', and expands the edges of our vision.

It is perhaps worth pondering that Jesus of Nazareth who invited people to commit to the struggle in the breaking of bread at the Last Supper was also recognised after death by the way in which he broke the bread they shared. There would appear to be significance here too for the Fat Jesus. As I have said, feminist liberation theology always understands Christology as ethical and so in speaking of recognition of Jesus after death I am not meaning to go into the metaphysical realm I have so roundly criticised throughout the book. What I am forced to ask is what is the ethical significance if any of this recognition? I think it is that we are reminded to invite all to the table, to celebrate the beauty in lives through ensuring that bodies are rested, well cared for and fed. Of course there is the undeniable reality that the world is patriarchal and that all the hierarchies that limit us are held in place through embodied practices and repeated acts of dis-embodiment and dismemberment. I have argued that the nature of the resurrection people, the pilgrim people, is that we rise again and again in the face of the repeated blasphemies of our world, each time moving and shifting the edges of what keeps us away from home. The controlled bodies of women are constant reminders of what is not yet here, the made up and abjected bodies of women are calls to rebellion. We need to be ever mindful of the way in which our fullness is limited but we also need to live the countercultural rebellion of the Fat Jesus.

And how will we know when the oppression of women is over? Well, when the Fat Jesus sings, of course!

Afterwords

Coffee and mints!

During the writing of this book there has been another great scientific discovery – the fat gene! In the last few years we have had the God gene, the gay gene and now the fat gene. An eminent professor appeared on the television to tell the world that he was delighted with this discovery since it allowed his diabetic patients to feel less guilty about their condition; it was not their fault now, it was a predisposition of which they had fallen foul. They need no longer feel lazy and gluttonous, rather they could feel unfortunate. It seems to me there is no more intimate way to dissolve politics than to embed them in the genetic make-up of individuals. This book has argued that what is made up to be a personal problem, a weakness, one that may even decide the moral character of the person who bears the weight, is in fact a highly politicised reality and should be approached as such in the way that we see it and react to it. Here we have perhaps the most emblematic explanation of our individualist advanced capitalist system, the human gene. The human gene takes the heat off – off the individual, yes, who does not have to be a figure of scorn and disgust but rather pity. This is an improvement when we have an incarnational starting point. However, it also takes the heat off the corporations, be they food or fitness and diet; food companies no longer have to look at the questions of the quality and price of food and can continue to pump steroids into 'meat' and sugar into low-fat, low-cost products. The food franchises do not have to think twice about getting their products into schools because it is only those students with the fat gene who will be adversely affected and they will be picked up by the caring sharing fitness and diet industries. The hard questions do not have to be faced: they can disappear in the soft flesh of the chosen, chosen, that is, to obscure the more toxic workings of society.

Of course it is not the thing to do to criticise the science that is, as we know, the most recent and most entrenched aspect of the medicalization of all social political issues. I am sure there are genes as described, but this finding in isolation and speaking as though it were the final word on the matter does not forward the cause of the outpouring of glorious incarnation through abundant life. Once again we have an extreme privatisation of what is in reality a social matter. The bodies of women, as we have seen, are speaking a profound reality, and to be silenced though a genetic argument is a step backwards. The God gene certainly allowed the matter of religion to become a rather unfortunate genetic curse, although 'research' has tried to rescue it by claiming that those who have it are calmer and live longer, but nevertheless belief within this scheme does become a matter that is even more fundamental than choice – it is in your make-up and you cannot help it. If you cannot help it then you do not have to be taken too seriously when you have it – a grand silencing technique. I think we can see this in the matter of religion. It may be a little harder for us to see in relation to the fat gene – after all, we may not be used to understanding the body and matters related to it as political. I hope this book has helped in that respect.

Notes

Epigraph
1. Lisa Isherwood and Elizabeth Stuart, *Introducing Body Theology* (Sheffield, Sheffield Academic Press, 1998), p. 60.

Introduction: Heaven is a room of fat women laughing!
1. See Susan Bordo, *Unbearable Weight: Feminism, Western Culture and the Body* (Berkeley, University of California Press, 1993), p. 5. The report about non-employment of overweight women by high street banks was a recent TV news item.
2. See www.ohpe.ca (Ontario Health Promotion E-Bulletin).
3. www.ohpe.ca.
4. www.ohpe.ca.
5. See Lisa Isherwood, *Liberating Christ* (Cleveland, Pilgrim Press, 1999).
6. See Marcella Althaus-Reid, *Indecent Theology* (London, Routledge, 2001).
7. Those who have read *Liberating Christ* will understand that this is far from the individualistic statement that it appears to be; it is rather a cry for heaven on earth, a cry both biblical and doctrinal. It is a call for the radical nature of incarnation to be taken seriously, to be lived, to be put on. I have my critics!
8. Pasi Falk, *The Consuming Body* (London, Sage, 1994), p. 20.
9. Falk, *The Consuming Body*, p. 21.
10. Falk, *The Consuming Body*, p. 25.
11. Falk, *The Consuming Body*, p. 34.

Chapter 1: The big question is: who let the skinny girls in?
1. Eve Ensler, *The Good Body* (London, William Heinemann, 2004), p. 20.
2. Simone de Beauvoir, quoted in Polly Young-Eisendrath, *Women and Desire: Beyond Wanting to Be Wanted* (London, Piatkus, 1999), p. 43.
3. Roberta Seid, 'Too Close to the Bone: The Historical Context for Women's Obsession with Slenderness' in Patricia Fallon, Melanie A. Katzman and Susan C. Wooley (eds), *Feminist Perspectives on Eating Disorders* (New York, Guilford Press, 1996), pp. 3–16 at p. 15.
4. Seid, 'Too Close', p. 8.
5. Naomi Wolf, 'Hunger' in Fallon, Katzman and Wooley (eds), *Feminist Perspectives*, pp. 94–111 at p. 99.
6. Wolf, 'Hunger', p. 98.
7. Wolf, 'Hunger', p. 99.
8. Wolf, 'Hunger', p. 110.

9. Ontario Health Promotion E–Bulletin, 'Ana and Mia': The Online World of Anorexia and Bulimia'.

10. http://news.bbc.co.uk/i/hi/health/3368833.stm, 'Teenage Girls "Hate Their Bodies"', accessed 7 February 2007.

11. Audre Lorde, 'The Master's Tools Will Never Dismantle the Master's House' in *Sister Outsider* (New York, Crossing Press, 1984), pp. 110–13.

12. This is the series that calls itself *Sex in the City* for lesbians, its publicity line being 'different city, same sex'.

13. Nelle Morton, *The Journey is Home* (Boston, Beacon Press, 1985).

14. Wolf, 'Hunger', p. 100.

15. Wolf, 'Hunger', p. 101.

16. Wolf, 'Hunger', p. 105.

17. Wolf, 'Hunger', p. 61.

18. James Nelson, *Body Theology* (Louisville, Westminster/John Knox Press, 1992), pp. 93–104.

19. Seid, 'Too Close', p. 13.

20. Joyce Huff, 'A Horror of Corpulence' in Jana Evans Braziel and Kathleen LeBesco (eds), *Bodies Out of Bounds: Fatness and Transgression* (Berkeley, University of California Press, 2001), pp. 39–59.

21. Susan Wooley, 'Sexual Abuse and Eating Disorders: The Concealed Debate' in Fallon, Katzman and Wooley (eds), *Feminist Perspectives*, pp. 171–211.

22. Rita Nakashima Brock, *Journeys by Heart: A Christology of Erotic Power* (New York, Crossroad, 1988).

23. Brock, *Journeys by Heart*, p. 17.

24. This may be a good time to point out that I am not suggesting that too much weight in some people cannot cause physical distress, but I am challenging the whole notion of 'too much'. It is unclear where that line is and for the most part it appears to be an individual matter.

25. Lisa Isherwood, *The Good News of the Body* (Sheffield, Sheffield Academic Press, 2000).

26. Susan Bordo, *Unbearable Weight: Feminism, Western Culture and the Body* (Berkeley, University of California Press, 1993), p. 208.

27. Kim Chernin, *Womansize: The Tyranny of Slenderness* (London, The Women's Press, 1983), p. 97.

28. Chernin, *Womansize*, p. 100.

29. Mary Daly, *Gyn/Ecology: The Metaethics of Radical Feminism* (Boston, Beacon Press, 1978).

30. Quoted in Huff, 'A Horror of Corpulence', p. 46.

31. Susie Orbach, *Fat Is a Feminist Issue* (London, Hamlyn Paperbacks, 1979).

32. Orbach, *Fat Is a Feminist Issue*, p. 18.

33. Catherine Steiner-Adair, 'The Politics of Prevention' in Fallon, Katzman and Wooley (eds), *Feminist Perspectives*, pp. 381–94.

34. Steiner-Adair, 'Politics', p. 390.

35. Steiner-Adair, 'Politics', p. 391.

36. Steiner-Adair, 'Politics', p. 250.
37. Judith Butler, *Bodies That Matter* (London, Routledge, 1993).
38. I do not wish to suggest that it is only Christianity that has created this body-policing rhetoric for women, but as a Christian theologian I can only speak with authenticity about that tradition.

Chapter 2: The gate is narrow: creating theological body boundaries
1. Elisabeth Moltmann-Wendel, *I Am My Body* (London, SCM Press, 1994), p. 105.
2. Quoted in Ken Stone, *Practicing Safer Texts* (London, T&T Clark, 2006), p. 27.
3. Stone, *Safer Texts*, p. 28.
4. Stone, *Safer Texts*, p. 35.
5. Stone, *Safer Texts*, p. 39.
6. Stone, *Safer Texts*, p. 11.
7. Judith Butler develops this idea in *Gender Trouble* (New York, Routledge, 1990).
8. Stone, *Safer Texts*, p. 50.
9. L. Shannon Jung, *Food For Life: The Spirituality and Ethics of Eating* (Minneapolis, Fortress Press, 2004), p. 24.
10. Stone, *Safer Texts*, p. 100.
11. Stone, *Safer Texts*, p. 101.
12. Stone, *Safer Texts*, p. 138.
13. Stephen Moore, *God's Gym* (London, Routledge, 1996), p. 94.
14. Moore, *God's Gym*, p. 89.
15. Moore, *God's Gym*, p. 139.
16. Walter Vandereycken and Ron Van Deth, *From Fasting Saints to Anorexic Girls: The History of Self-Starvation* (London, Athlone Press, 1996), p. 35.
17. Vandereycken and Van Deth, *Fasting Saints*, p. 22.
18. Vandereycken and Van Deth, *Fasting Saints*, p. 37.
19. Vandereycken and Van Deth, *Fasting Saints*, p. 41.
20. Vandereycken and Van Deth, *Fasting Saints*, p. 47.
21. Rudolf Bell, *Holy Anorexia* (Chicago, University of Chicago Press, 1987).
22. Caroline Walker Bynum, *Holy Feast, Holy Fast: The Religious Significance of Food to Medieval Women* (Berkeley, University of California Press, 1987), p. 31.
23. Walker Bynum, *Holy Feast*, p. 150.
24. Walker Bynum, *Holy Feast*, p. 157.
25. Walker Bynum, *Holy Feast*, p. 209.
26. See also Caroline Walker Bynum, *Jesus as Mother: Studies in the Spirituality of the High Middle Ages* (Los Angeles, University of California Press, 1982), *passim*.
27. Walker Bynum, *Holy Feast*, p. 272.
28. Walker Bynum, *Holy Feast*, p. 271.
29. Walker Bynum, *Holy Feast*, p. 112.

30. Caroline Walker Bynum, *Fragmentation and Redemption: Essays on Gender and the Human Body in Medieval Religion* (New York, Zed Books, 1991), p. 102.
31. Walker Bynum, *Jesus as Mother*, p. 293.
32. See Lisa Isherwood, 'Indecent Theology: What F—ing Difference Does It Make?', *Feminist Theology* Vol. 11 No. 2 (January 2003), pp. 141–7.
33. Walker Bynum, *Holy Feast*, p. 298.
34. R. Marie Griffith, *Born Again Bodies: Flesh and Spirit in American Christianity* (Berkeley, University of California Press, 2004), p. 31.
35. Griffith, *Born Again Bodies*, p. 37.
36. Griffith, *Born Again Bodies*, p. 40.
37. Griffith, *Born Again Bodies*, p. 44.
38. Griffith, *Born Again Bodies*, p. 111. Elizabeth Towne (b. 1860) was a publisher of her own and other's books, mostly on self-improvement topics of interest to those drawn to New Thought.
39. Griffith, *Born Again Bodies*, p. 113.
40. Griffith, *Born Again Bodies*, p. 217.
41. Griffith, *Born Again Bodies*, p. 117.
42. Griffith, *Born Again Bodies*, pp. 142–3.
43. As a counter to my own argument I have to add that in conversation with some Womanist friends they have put forward quite an opposite view, that in slavery black people were 'bred big' in order to be able to carry out the heavy work and so contemporary women particularly are taking the slimming option to show autonomy. Is this too a political argument for giving in to the slender world?
44. See Lisa Isherwood, *The Power of Erotic Celibacy* (London, T&T Clark, 2006).

Chapter 3: 'Slim For Him'

1. The 'Slim For Him' programme is a specific weight-loss programme developed in the USA within an evangelical theological frame, but it serves here in a more general sense to illustrate the purpose of this chapter which is to look at how weight loss and religion have interplayed over the last 150 years or so.
2. Simone de Beauvoir, quoted in Kim Chernin, *Womansize: The Tyranny of Slenderness* (London, The Women's Press, 1983), p. 66.
3. Sian Busby, *A Wonderful Little Girl* (London, Short Books, 2003), p. 42.
4. Busby, *A Wonderful Little Girl*, p. 50.
5. Walter Vandereycken and Ron Van Deth, *From Fasting Saints to Anorexic Girls: The History of Self Starvation* (London, Athlone Press, 1996), p. 186.
6. Michelle Mary Lelwica, *Starving for Salvation: The Spiritual Dimension of Eating Problems among American Girls and Women* (Oxford, Oxford University Press, 1999), p. 29.
7. Lelwica, *Starving for Salvation*, p. 72. William Banting wrote the first low-carbohydrate diet book, published in 1863.

8. Mary Douglas, *Collected Works, Vol. III: Natural Symbols* (London, Routledge, 2003), p. xii, quoted in Lelwica, *Starving for Salvation*, p. 44.

9. Lelwica, *Starving for Salvation*, p. 42.

10. Lelwica, *Starving for Salvation*, p. 94.

11. Griffith, *Born Again Bodies*, p. 166.

12. Griffith, *Born Again Bodies*, p. 168.

13. Griffith, *Born Again Bodies*, p. 170.

14. Griffith, *Born Again Bodies*, p. 178.

15. Griffith, *Born Again Bodies*, p. 183.

16. Griffith, *Born Again Bodies*, p. 177.

17. Griffith, *Born Again Bodies*, p. 180.

18. See my analysis of this in *The Power of Erotic Celibacy* (London, T&T Clark, 2006), ch. 4, in which I suggest that this is a politically and financially based programme that has little if anything to do with the Christ of the gospels.

19. This is the corporate God who has been emerging for some decades now with the push to kill off the liberation theology discourse which was spearheaded from the USA because the God of liberation theology was causing too much international unrest: people were beginning to understand the mechanics of their desperate situations and to ask that they should change.

20. Griffith, *Born Again Bodies*, p. 209.

21. Griffith, *Born Again Bodies*, p. 217.

22. Griffith, *Born Again Bodies*, p. 223.

23. Griffith, *Born Again Bodies*, p. 221. The verses are from the Song of Songs (Song of Solomon) 4:1a, 6b, 7.

24. Nancy L. Eiesland, *The Disabled God: Toward a Liberatory Theology of Disability* (Nashville, Abingdon Press, 1994), p. 99.

25. Elizabeth Stuart, 'Disruptive Bodies: Disability, Embodiment and Sexuality' in Lisa Isherwood (ed.), *The Good News of the Body: Sexual Theology and Feminism* (Sheffield, Sheffield Academic Press, 2000), pp. 166–84.

26. Griffith, *Born Again Bodies*, p. 1

27. www.rebeccamead.com/2001/2001_01_15_art_slim.htm, p. 1.

28. www.rebeccamead.com/2001/2001_01_15_art_slim.htm, p. 3.

29. www.rebeccamead.com/2001/2001_01_15_art_slim.htm, p. 7.

30. See Lisa Isherwood, *The Power of Erotic Celibacy* (London, T&T Clark, 2006).

31. www.rebeccamead.com/2001/2001_01_15_art_slim.htm, p. 3.

32. Accessible through www.cust.idl.com.au/fold/Deepthoughts_index.html.

33. www.cust.idl.com.au/no fatties in heaven, p. 3.

34. See Doris Buss and Didi Herman, *Globalizing Family Values: The Christian Right in International Politics* (Minneapolis, University of Minnesota Press, 2003).

35. Griffith, *Born Again Bodies*, p. 225.
36. Susan Bordo, quoted in Griffith, *Born Again Bodies*, p. 225.
37. See Lisa Isherwood, *Liberating Christ* (Cleveland, Pilgrim Press, 1999).
38. Lisa Isherwood, 'The Embodiment of Feminist Liberation Theology: The Spiralling of Incarnation' in *Embodying Feminist Liberation Theologies*, ed. Beverley Clack (London, T&T Clark, 2003), pp. 140–56.
39. See Lisa Isherwood, *Introducing Feminist Christologies* (London, Continuum, 2001).
40. Quoted in Griffith, *Born Again Bodies*, p. 227.
41. See Marcella Althaus-Reid, *Indecent Theology: Theological Perversions in Sex, Gender and Politcs* (London, Routledge, 2001).
42. Griffith, *Born Again Bodies*, p. 230.
43. Griffith, *Born Again Bodies*, p. 232.
44. Griffith, *Born Again Bodies*, p. 242.
45. Griffith, *Born Again Bodies*, p. 243.
46. See www.TrueLoveWaits.com.

Chapter 4: Women and desire: cream cakes, champagne and orgasms

1. Polly Young-Eisendrath, *Women and Desire: Beyond Wanting to Be Wanted* (London, Piatkus, 1999), p. 50.
2. Cecilia Hartley, 'Letting Ourselves Go: Making Room for the Fat Body in Feminist Scholarship' in Jana Evans Braziel and Kathleen LeBesco (eds), *Bodies Out of Bounds: Fatness and Transgression* (Berkeley, University of California Press, 2001), pp. 60–73, at p. 62.
3. Hartley, 'Letting Ouselves Go', p. 72.
4. Naomi Wolf, 'Hunger' in P. Fallon, M. A. Katzman and S. C. Wooley (eds), *Feminist Perspectives on Eating Disorders* (New York, Guilford Press, 1994), pp. 94–111, at p. 98.
5. Monique Wittig, 'The Straight Mind', *Feminist Issues* Vol. 1, No. 1 (Summer 1980), p. 105.
6. Wittig, 'The Straight Mind', p. 106.
7. Mary Daly, *Pure Lust and Elemental Feminist Philosophy* (London, The Women's Press, 1988), p. 84.
8. Hartley, 'Letting Ourselves Go', p. 65.
9. Helena Mitchie, *The Flesh Made Word: Female Figures and Women's Bodies* (New York, Oxford University Press, 1987), quoted in Susan Bordo, *Unbearable Weight: Feminism, Western Culture and the Body* (Berkeley, University of California, 1993), p. 183.
10. Lisa Isherwood (ed.), *The Good News of the Body* (Sheffield, Sheffield Academic Press, 2000).
11. Kim Chernin, *Womansize: The Tyranny of Slenderness* (London, The Women's Press, 1983), p. 32.
12. Chernin, *Womansize*, p.120.
13. Chernin, *Womansize*, p. 125.
14. Chernin, *Womansize*, p. 141. Dorothy Dinnerstein's work referred to is

The Rocking of the Cradle and the Ruling of the World (New York, Harper & Row, 1977).

15. Chernin, *Womansize*, p. 74.
16. Chernin, *Womansize*, p. 80.
17. Haunani-Kay Trask, *Eros and Power: The Promise of Feminist Theory* (Philadelphia, University of Pennsylvania Press, 1986), p. 29.
18. Adrienne Rich, from 'Sibling Mysteries' in *The Dream of a Common Language*, quoted in Trask, *Eros and Power*, p. 106.
19. Chernin, *Womansize*, p. 148.
20. Michelle Mary Lelwica, *Starving For Salvation: The Spiritual Dimension of Eating Problems among American Girls and Women* (Oxford, Oxford University Press, 1999), p. 26.
21. Chernin, *Womansize*, p. 109.
22. Robin Morgan, *Lady of the Beasts* (New York, Random House, 1976), pp. 87–8.
23. Trask, *Eros and Power*, p. 173.
24. Trask, *Eros and Power*, p. 136.
25. Trask, *Eros and Power*, p. 139.
26. Jessica Benjamin, 'Master and Slave: The Fantasy of Erotic Domination' in Ann Snitow (ed.), *Powers of Desire* (New York, Monthly Review Press, 1983), pp. 75–127, at p. 77.
27. Benjamin, 'Master and Slave', p. 88.
28. Benjamin, 'Master and Slave', p. 126.
29. Benjamin, 'Master and Slave', p. 127.
30. Young-Eisendrath, *Women and Desire*, p. 43.
31. Young-Eisendrath, *Women and Desire*, p. 42.
32. Young-Eisendrath, *Women and Desire*, p. 48.
32. Young-Eisendrath, *Women and Desire*, p. 62.
33. Young-Eisendrath, *Women and Desire*, p. 40.
34. Carter Heyward, *The Redemption of God* (Washington, University of America Press, 1982).
35. Lisa Isherwood, *Liberating Christ* (Cleveland, Pilgrim Press, 1999).
36. Heyward, *Redemption of God*, p. 25.
37. Heyward, *Redemption of God*, p. 48.
38. Catherine Garrett, *Beyond Anorexia: Narrative, Spirituality and Recovery* (Cambridge, Cambridge University Press, 1998), p. 57.
39. Jo Ind, *Fat Is a Spiritual Issue* (London, Mowbray, 1993).
40. Ind, *Fat Is a Spiritual Issue*, p. 4.
41. Garrett, *Beyond Anorexia*, p. 115.
42. Garrett, *Beyond Anorexia*, p. 110.
43. Chernin, *Womansize*, p. 108.
44. I personally do not just hear these words in terms of physical size alone, although I welcome that celebration wholeheartedly, but I do not wish to be seen as imposing the huge body on to women – this would simply be another imposition. What I long for is the hugeness of women living

fully, abundantly and expansively in their skins with an unrestricted sense of life. I long for us to dream it and live it.

45. Chernin, *Womansize*, p. 78.

Chapter 5: Breaking bread with ourselves

1. Susie Orbach, *Fat Is a Feminist Issue* (London: Hamlyn Paperbacks, 1979), p. 24.
2. M. M. Lelwica, *Starving for Salvation: The Spiritual Dimension of Eating Problems among American Girls and Women* (Oxford, Oxford University Press, 1999), p. 68.
3. Lelwica, *Starving for Salvation*, p. 69.
4. Lelwica, *Starving for Salvation*, p. 75.
5. Lelwica, *Starving for Salvation*, p. 78.
6. Kandi Stinson, *Women and Dieting Culture: Inside a Commercial Weight Loss Group* (New Brunswick, Rutgers University Press, 2001).
7. Stinson, *Women and Dieting Culture*, p. 9.
8. See Max Weber, *Protestantism and the Spirit of Capitalism* (1904) for more on this.
9. Stinson, *Women and Dieting Culture*, p. 52.
10. Stinson, *Women and Dieting Culture*, p. 53.
11. Stinson, *Women and Dieting Culture*, p. 54.
12. Rita Nakashima Brock, *Journeys by Heart: A Christology of Erotic Power* (New York, Crossroad, 1988), p. 17.
13. Brock, *Journeys by Heart*, p. 40.
14. Stinson, *Women and Dieting Culture*, p. 127.
15. Stinson, *Women and Dieting Culture*, p. 156.
16. Stinson, *Women and Dieting Culture*, p. 160.
17. Greg Critser, *Fat Land: How Americans Became the Fattest People in the World* (London, Penguin, 2003), p. 39.
18. L. Shannon Jung, *Food for Life: The Spirituality and Ethics of Eating* (Minneapolis, Fortress Press, 2004), p. 87.
19. Jung, *Food for Life*, p. 63.
20. Tissa Balasuriya, *The Eucharist and Human Liberation* (London, SPCK, 1988).
21. Jung, *Food for Life*, p. 14.
22. Jung, *Food for Life*, p. 6.
23. Jung, *Food for Life*, p. 8.
24. Jung, *Food for Life*, p. 49.
25. Richard Klein, 'Fat Beauty' in J. E. Braziel and Kathleen LeBesco (eds), *Out of Bounds: Fatness and Transgression* (Berkeley, University of California Press, 2001), p. 21.
26. Klein, 'Fat Beauty', p. 22.
27. Klein, 'Fat Beauty', p. 35.
28. Katherine Hayle (author of *How We Became Post-Human*), quoted in R. Marie Griffith, *Born Again Bodies: Flesh and Spirit in American Christianity*

(Berkeley, University of California Press, 2004), p. 249.

29. Klein, 'Fat Beauty', p. 3.
30. Marcella Althaus-Reid, *Indecent Theology: Theological Perversions in Sex, Gender and Politics* (London, Routledge, 2001), p. 111.

Bibliography

Althaus-Reid, Marcella, *Indecent Theology: Theological Perversions in Sex, Gender and Politcs*, London, Routledge, 2001.

Balasuriya, Tissa, *The Eucharist and Human Liberation*, London, SPCK, 1988.

Bell, Rudolf, *Holy Anorexia*, Chicago, University of Chicago Press, 1987.

Benjamin, Jessica, 'Master and Slave: The Fantasy of Erotic Domination' in Ann Snitow (ed.), *Powers of Desire*, New York, Monthly Review Press, 1983, pp. 75–127.

Bordo, Susan, *Unbearable Weight: Feminism, Western Culture and the Body*, Berkeley, University of California Press, 1993.

Braziel, Jana Evans and LeBesco, Kathleen (eds), *Bodies Out oOf Bounds: Fatness and Transgression*, Berkeley, University of California Press, 2001.

Brock, Rita Nakashima, *Journeys by Heart: A Christology of Erotic Power*, New York, Crossroad, 1988.

Busby, Sian, *A Wonderful Little Girl*, London, Short Books, 2003.

Buss, Doris and Didi, Herman, *Globalizing Family Values: The Christian Right in International Politics*, Minneapolis, University of Minnesota Press, 2003.

Butler, Judith, *Bodies That Matter*, London, Routledge, 1993.

Chernin, Kim, *Womansize: The Tyranny of Slenderness*, London, The Women's Press, 1983.

Critser, Greg, *Fat Land: How Americans Became the Fattest People in the World*, London, Penguin, 2003.

Daly, Mary, *Pure Lust and Elemental Feminist Philosophy*, London, The Women's Press, 1988.

Dinnerstein, Dorothy, *The Rocking of the Cradle and the Ruling of the World*, New York, Harper & Row, 1977.

Eiesland, Nancy L., *The Disabled God: Toward a Liberatory Theology of Disability*, Nashville, Abingdon Press, 1994.

Ensler, Eve, *The Good Body*, London, William Heinemann, 2004.

Falk, Pasi, *The Consuming Body*, London, Sage, 1994.

Fallon, Patricia, Katzman, Melanie A. and Wooley, Susan C. (eds), *Feminist Perspectives on Eating Disorders*, New York, The Guilford Press, 1994.

Garrett, Catherine, *Beyond Anorexia: Narrative, Spirituality and Recovery*, Cambridge, Cambridge University Press, 1998.

Griffith, R. Marie, *Born Again Bodies. Flesh and Spirit in American Christianity*, Berkeley, University of California Press, 2004.

Hartley, Cecilia, 'Letting Ourselves Go: Making Room for the Fat Body in Feminist Scholarship' in Braziel and LeBesco (eds), *Bodies Out of Bounds*, pp. 60–73.

Heyward, Carter, *The Redemption of God*, Washington, University of America Press, 1982.

Huff, Joyce, 'A Horror of Corpulence' in Braziel and LeBesco (eds), *Bodies Out Of Bounds*, pp. 39–59.

Ind, Jo, *Fat Is a Spiritual Issue*, London, Mowbray, 1993.

Isherwood, Lisa and Stuart, Elizabeth, *Introducing Body Theology*, Sheffield, Sheffield Academic Press, 1998.

Isherwood, Lisa, *Liberating Christ*, Cleveland, Pilgrim Press, 1999.

Isherwood, Lisa (ed.), *The Good News of the Body*, Sheffield, Sheffield Academic Press, 2000.

Isherwood, Lisa, *Introducing Feminist Christologies*, London, Continuum, 2001.

Isherwood, Lisa, 'The Embodiment of Feminist Liberation Theology: The Spiralling of Incarnation' in Beverley Clack (ed.), *Embodying Feminist Liberation Theologies*, London, T&T Clark, 2003, pp. 140–56.

Isherwood, Lisa, *The Power of Erotic Celibacy*, London, T&T Clark, 2006.

Jung, L. Shannon, *Food For Life: The Spirituality and Ethics of Eating*, Minneapolis, Fortress Press, 2004.

Klein, Richard, 'Fat Beauty' in Braziel and LeBesco (eds), *Bodies Out of Bounds*, pp. 119–38.

Lelwica, Michelle Mary, *Starving for Salvation: The Spiritual Dimension of Eating Problems among American Girls and Women*, Oxford, Oxford University Press, 1999.

Mitchie, Helena, *The Flesh Made Word: Female Figures and Women's Bodies*, New York, Oxford University Press, 1987.

Moltmann-Wendel, Elisabeth, *I Am My Body*, London, SCM Press, 1994.

Moore, Stephen, *God's Gym*, London, Routledge, 1996.

Morgan, Robin, *Lady of the Beasts*, New York, Random House, 1976.

Morton, Nelle, *The Journey is Home*, Boston, Beacon Press, 1985.

Nelson, James, *Body Theology*, Louisville, Westminster John Knox Press, 1992.

Orbach, Susie, *Fat Is a Feminist Issue*, London, Hamlyn Paperbacks, 1979.

Seid, Roberta, 'Too Close to the Bone: The Historical Context for Women's Obsession with Slenderness' in Fallon, Katzman and Wooley (eds), *Feminist Perspectives on Eating Disorders*, pp. 3–16.

Steiner-Adair, Catherine, 'The Politics of Prevention' in Fallon, Katzman and Wooley (eds), *Feminist Perspectives on Eating Disorders*, pp. 381–94.

Stinson, Kandi, *Women and Dieting Culture: Inside a Commercial Weight Loss Group*, New Brunswick, Rutgers University Press, 2001.

Stone, Ken, *Practicing Safer Texts*, London, T&T Clark , 2006.

Stuart, Elizabeth, 'Disruptive Bodies: Disability, Embodiment and Sexuality' in Isherwood (ed.), *The Good News of the Body*, pp. 166–84.

'Teenage Girls "Hate Their Bodies"' at http://news.bbc.co.uk/i/hi/health/3368833.stm, accessed 7 February 2007.

Trask, Haunani-Kay, *Eros and Power: The Promise of Feminist Theory*, Philadelphia, University of Pennsylvania Press, 1986.

Vandereycken, Walter and Van Deth, Ron, *From Fasting Saints to Anorexic*

Girls: The History of Self Starvation, London, Athlone Press, 1996.

Walker Bynum, Caroline, *Jesus as Mother: Studies in the Spirituality of the High Middle Ages*, Los Angeles, University of California Press, 1982.

Walker Bynum, Caroline, *Holy Feast, Holy Fast: The Religious Significance of Food to Medieval Women*, Berkeley, University of California Press, 1987.

Wittig, Monique, 'The Straight Mind', *Feminist Issues* Vol. 1, No. 1, Summer 1980.

Wolf, Naomi, 'Hunger' in Fallon, Katzman and Wooley (eds), *Feminist Perspectives on Eating Disorders*, pp. 94–111.

Wooley, Susan, 'Sexual Abuse and Eating Disorders: The Concealed Debate' in Fallon, Katzman and Wooley (eds), *Feminist Perspectives on Eating Disorders*, pp. 171–211.

www.cust.idl.com.au/fold/Deepthoughts_index.html

www.rebeccamead.com/2001/2001_01_15_art_slim.htm

www.TrueLoveWaits.com

Young-Eisendrath, Polly, *Women and Desire: Beyond Wanting to Be Wanted*, London, Piatkus, 1999.

Index